Beyond Contradiction

Essays for Peace and Justice

in memory of Paul Baker

1954 — 1989

ESSAYS IN MEMORY OF

DAVID PAUL BAKER
1954 — 1989

Published by Paul Baker Estate
    13 Fremantle Square, Kingsdown
    Bristol BS6 8TL

ISBN 0 9520265 0 3

Printed in Great Britain by
    Cliftonprint, 21 Clifton Road,
    Clifton, Bristol BS8 1AE

CONTRIBUTORS

Canon Alastair Redfern   Canon Theologian, Diocese of Bristol.

Dr. Gill Cox   G.P., widow of Paul Baker.

Mick Fleming   Chairperson of the Knowle West Community Association.

Dr. Paul Joyce   Lecturer in Old Testament, Department of Theology, University of Birmingham.

Angela West   Christian feminist writer and English teacher.

Fr. Roger Ruston   Lecturer in Christian Ethics, Department of Theology, University of Bristol.

The Rt. Revd. Rowan Williams   Bishop of Monmouth. Formerly Lady Margaret Professor of Divinity, Oxford.

Doctor Una Kroll   Physician, Counsellor, writer and contemplative nun, Society of the Sacred Cross.

Revd. Andrew Hake   Retired Social Development Officer, Borough of Thamesdown. Member of the Archbishop's Commission on Faith in the City.

Very Revd. Horace Dammers   Founder of the Life-Style Movement. Dean Emeritus of Bristol.

Revd. Sue Walrond-Skinner   Adviser in Pastoral Care and Counselling. Diocese of Southwark.

CONTENTS

Preface   **Alastair Redfern**

Paul Baker

Paul Baker died suddenly and unexpectedly on March 11, 1989. He was only thirty-four. I was privileged to know Paul as a theological student in Oxford, and then as a colleague in the Diocese of Bristol. To me, as to many others, he offered both encouragement and challenge in facing the demands of christian discipleship in the modern world.

Preaching on Martin Luther King Day in 1984 Paul said:

"A disciple is someone who finds the life of Jesus in some way significant for their own life. Christian discipleship is a process of reflection and action in which the disciple relates their life to Jesus' life. Reflection must lead to action based on the teaching of Jesus. Action must lead to reflection on the activity of Jesus. This is the ebb and flow of discipleship — the dynamic which propels the life of the disciple.

Jesus taught us to love our neighbours as ourselves. Indeed Jesus went beyond the Old Testament commandment and enjoined us to love our enemies. Now love which goes as far as love for the enemy must put the security of the other before its own security. In consistently living out this ideal Jesus was prepared to make himself vulnerable. Vulnerable to the point of crucifixion. To the world such vulnerability appears as weakness, but it is in reality a new kind of power.

Jesus had no home he could call his own. He had no official status in his country or his religion. Apparently a complete lack of security and power. But Jesus did have confidence in God. And this gave him a new security and a new power. The freedom and courage with which Jesus criticised the civil and religious authorities of his day can only be understood as a result of such spiritual power ... We too must make ourselves vulnerable. To accept the vulnerability which lies at the heart of christian discipleship requires courage. God gives us courage. Only the disciple who risks losing his or her life will gain it. God gives us courage, but we must risk losing our life. This is the promise and challenge of Jesus to his disciples.''

Those words describe a vision, a confidence, a sense of urgency, a model of action which Paul brought to a wide range of issues facing the contemporary church — peace and violence, social injustice, the environment, sexuality, apartheid. In all these areas Paul made a vigorous contribution, from his gentle work with countless individuals to his courageous public appeals in church councils and synods and in the political and community structures.

The essays in this book are contributed by some of Paul's fellow disciples. They aim to continue to challenge us in each of the areas in which Paul was so deeply engaged. Most of the contributors had a close personal contact with Paul and share our concern to commemorate him by continuing to call others to a more radical discipleship.

The compilation of this book has been the responsibility of Gill Cox, Sue Walrond-Skinner and myself. We are grateful to so many distinguished people for their contributions and for their patience with our editorial efforts.

These essays are offered as a tribute to a much loved friend and colleague, in the firm conviction that to continue to challenge and campaign for God's kingdom is a call to that which is truly beyond contradiction, and known to most of us in our better moments.

I hope that many other disciples may be inspired to think more deeply, to struggle more openly for the things of the Gospel and to trust more fully in the God whose own vulnerability is the source of supreme security and power.

Alastair Redfern

Section One

INTRODUCTION: A profile of Paul Baker
Gill Cox

"Indeed if you want to know what my Christian faith is all about, do not ask me about matters of biblical interpretation, of theological disputes or ecclesiastical preferences but instead, ask me about my vision of the Promised Land, of a world where there are no more divisions between rich and poor, black and white, east and west, women and men — of a time when men and women can join hands around the world in peace".

Paul preached these words outside the gates of the United States Air Force Base at Upper Heyford at Pentecost 1984, and in many ways they sum up his life. He had a vision and he worked single-mindedly to help it to come about. His theological views changed over the years from those of a conservative Evangelical to being in sympathy with Cupitt but these were really peripheral to his belief that if Christianity meant anything, it was about bringing Good News to the poor and turning swords into ploughshares. For Paul, "the world is not under God's thumb but in the inter-play between order and disorder there is always hope. In the world God wills the coming of a Kingdom of peace and justice and we are called to make this Kingdom a present reality".

Paul had decided to study physics at University partly because he thought it held the key to understanding the universe and the meaning of human existence but, although he retained a keen interest in science throughout his life, his search for understanding soon led in other directions and he became a Christian. This for him, however, was not the final answer but merely the beginning of more explorations into what being a Christian really meant. His initial critical thinking was mostly theological in nature but he came to appreciate that theology could not be carried out in a sociological vacuum. Later, speaking on the "Faith in the City" Report, he said "If the Church is to overcome the sense of alienation it has to show people that it is with them, where they are in practical ways ... The Church is not an ark in which a few might find safety from the swirling waters round about. The Gospel we proclaim is a broad message of hope to all and not salvation for a few".

His own practical response to the needs of the world was initially to consider becoming a medical physicist but then, during a serious illness, he confronted the possibility of an early death. This imported a sense of urgency to his life which never left him. He wrote "We have to come to terms with the fact that life is always moving towards death ... Life is always experienced with its face set towards death. Thus, while we may be unable to embrace death and to look forward to it, we need to see it as part of life, as a genuine pointer to the kind of existence that is ours." A previously vague sense of calling to the ministry was sharpened and he said he felt that God had met him in an unexpected place — that of suffering, and pointed him in a new direction.

Prior to going to theological college he spent a year working with homeless alcoholics in Spitalfields, East London. Although he had thought about issues of poverty and powerlessness before, this was probably his first real experience of it and he continued to reflect on it while doing a theology degree. His next experience of alienation however, came from an initially surprising source, from some of the women on his theological course. He later wrote, "My own initial reaction to being presented with women's issues was one of mild irritation. I felt I was a reasonably good lad with a reasonably oiled social conscience. For a long time, I considered women were of secondary importance to issues such as human rights, famine in Africa and the Bomb. It is only by listening to them that I have come to change..." In fact he listened well enough to be able to identify with the pain of those women whose calling to the priesthood was not yet recognised by the Church and to decide that he should stand in solidarity with them and not be ordained himself. In addition, he increasingly felt it to be a handicap, to be closely identified with the Institutional Church particularly in a priestly role and so he became a licensed lay worker when he left college and went to work in Knowle West, a run-down council estate on the edge of Bristol. Here he helped enable those of lower social standing to have more say in the running of the Church — for example by encouraging them to be elected onto the PCC. After this change in emphasis, the Church was ready to begin to move outward into the community and to use its premises as part of a local unemployment initiative. Sadly, things went wrong and Paul and his colleagues were subjected to much abuse as they tried to expose the apparent corruption of those running the scheme for their own political ends.

At other levels also Paul tried to give those who regard themselves as powerless, a voice. He helped start an Association of Urban Priority Area Parishes, partly in order to confront a Diocese which would really rather have liked to sweep the problems of parishes such as Knowle West under the carpet with philanthropic gestures. Paul always stood slightly aside from the Institutional Church in that he

3

did not want, and maybe would not have enjoyed, the comfortable life of fitting in with the powers that be and accepting only cosmetic improvements in the face of overwhelming injustice. In many ways his was a prophetic role, constantly challenging people in a disarmingly polite but persistent way, reminding them that Jesus spent much of his ministry confronting people and that we are called to love our enemies, not agree with them. On one occasion he wrote, "The pilgrim and pioneering people of God will not always be travelling in directions which bring respect and honour. Obedience to God will sometimes lead to a prophetic witness which only brings scorn and rejection. "Let us go forth to him outside the camp and bear the abuse he endured" (Hebrews Ch.13. v.13). The marks of such suffering are the marks of Jesus which are to characterise the people of God. Only such marks are appropriate within the community of Jesus' disciples and only the marks of such suffering open the community to the creative possibility of the world to come."

At Diocesan level Paul challenged those who thought it was acceptable to raise money from firms involved in South Africa, armaments and tobacco saying that the Church was called to be prophetic as well as pastoral and that only those in positions of relative wealth, power and privilege — like the majority of members of the Bristol Diocesan Synod, were likely to indulge in the fanciful theory of neutral money. (See the following paper).

Paul was always inspired by Jesus' totally peaceful but at the same time fully active resistance to evil and this led him to be arrested on several occasions and once to be briefly imprisoned (for refusal to pay the fine imposed by the court) for actions designed to demonstrate the evil involved in preparing for nuclear war. At one of his court appearances, he made the following statement, "I have pleaded guilty to breaking a minor law. But at a higher level, I believe Ash Wednesday was one of the least guilty days of my life. For instead of ignoring unpalatable facts, I was demonstrating opposition to the preparations being made for committing the greatest of crimes. On Ash Wednesday, I crossed the barbed wire fence of the US Air Force Base at Upper Heyford with nine others. Chained together in a circle, we celebrated Ash Wednesday, with readings, hymns and prayers, sprinkled ashes on each other and on the runway. This was an act of penance for our own sins and the suffering caused in past wars. Of course, celebrating Ash Wednesday inside the base rather than in a church introduced a political significance to our act of worship. We were calling on all governments to repent and turn back from the path of destruction which is the nuclear arms race."

Symbolic actions inside and outside bases, however, were only one way of getting the message across and Paul also helped initiate annual Ash Wednesday processions in the centre of Bristol where Christians of all denominations gathered to call for repentance and a change of heart by the government, so that more might be spent on Aid and less on Arms. In the last year of his life he was able, as a member of General

4

Synod, to move an amendment to a motion on "Peace making in a nuclear age". This amendment succeeded in sharpening up a paragraph urging the government to take all necessary initiatives to achieve a major reduction in nuclear and conventional armaments, by stressing the need for a comprehensive test ban treaty and of disengaging from "Star Wars". Paul would rather have moved a motion enjoining abandonment of British nuclear weapons but he recognised that compromise was sometimes necessary in order to achieve even small gains.

Paul died very suddenly at the age of 34. At the time of his death he was thinking of becoming a community worker and was doing a part-time course at the University. He wrote that he felt a bit more integrated doing a course on social policy and living in Knowle West than when he had lived in Brick Lane (Spitalfields) and was trying to write up his Physics PhD. In a way that was what he was trying to do all his life — to match up his intellectual reflection with the practical actions necessary to stand alongside the oppressed. He once wrote "Our solidarity with the poor in our parishes will lead to tensions in the Koinonia of the wider church where such solidarity is not a priority or even to be desired. In view of the polarities of wealth and poverty which exist in Britain today, solidarity with the poor and alienation from parts of the Church go hand in hand. How are we to handle the tensions and conflicts inherent in this solidarity and this alienation?. How indeed? And the question relates not only to the poor, but also to women, to the third world, to homosexuals, to creation itself... This book of essays is produced partly to honour the memory of Paul but its main aim is to continue to encourage reflection on some of the issues about which he cared so deeply.

SPEECH TO
THE BRISTOL DIOCESAN SYNOD
22ND NOVEMBER 1986 IN SUPPORT OF
THE MOTION BEFORE IT.

Paul Baker

RESOLUTION FOR BRISTOL DIOCESAN SYNOD (NOVEMBER 1986)

Ethical considerations for the Diocesan Development Programme's (DDP) appeal to industry and commerce

'This Synod notes the recent resolution of General Synod on South Africa (1) and resolves that the DDP's appeal to industry and commerce will not approach the 'top ten' UK companies currently involved in that country (2).

Recognizing the moral dilemmas facing the church in a complex world, this Synod nevertheless asks the DDP Committee to adhere to the well tried social and ethical criteria used by the Church Commissioners (3) when raising money from local commerce and industry.'

(1)   The July meeting of the General Synod of the Church of England voted overwhelmingly to request 'all bodies with significant links in South Africa, to take whatever steps are in their power — including acts of disengagement — to increase the pressure on that economy, and **urges the church's financial bodies to give a clear lead in this direction.'**

(2)   The 'top ten' are: Barclays and Standard Banks, Shell, BP, GEC, ICI, RTZ, Consolidated Goldfields, British Tyre and Rubber, BOC.

(3)   The Church Commissioners 'do not invest in companies whose main business is in armaments, gambling, breweries and distilleries, tobacco and newspapers.'

Proposer: Dr Paul Baker
Seconder: Revd. Melvyn Matthews

This motion was debated because the Diocese of Bristol was proposing to approach local industry for donations to its Diocesan Development Programme. No ethical guidelines had been drawn up and none were officially adopted since this motion was defeated.

THE MOTION:

When you read the motion before you I am sure many of you felt you were being asked to peer into Pandora's box. Apartheid, war, lung cancer...an almost endless list of horrors and complicated problems. But at its heart lies the simple concern that the values of the gospel should not fly out of the window when we enter the market place.

Industry and commerce are not some neutral territory lying outside the sphere of God's redemptive action and purpose. This appeal for money is not an area of immunity from the commandment to love our neighbour : on the contrary it is a specific opportunity to put our words into action.

As Christians we are committed to an ethical pilgrimage. When we commit ourselves to belief in a God of Love we embrace a way of life. Our relationship to God has no meaning apart from our relationship to other human beings. 'He who says he is in the light and hates his brother is in the darkness still'.

The way is full of difficult choices. We shall make mistakes, but moral laziness is the only mortal sin. The excuse 'it's all too difficult'' is the only path to perdition. So industry and commerce must not be allowed to slip out of the moral arena. To do so would hand over an important area of God given human work and endeavour to a selfish and materialistically centred exploitation of human beings and the rest of God's creation. To refuse to consider such issues would be an abdication of our responsibility to be a sign of God's presence everywhere, the light of the world, a city set on a hill which cannot be hid.

There can be no doubt that ethical considerations must play a part in our appeal to industry. Indeed I suspect that some areas of moral awareness are so deeply rooted in our consciences that some ethical guidelines would automatically come into play even without this debate. For example I am sure we would all be very surprised if our Development Committee approached a chain of sex shops. And quite rightly they would not go to such a source for funds. Eureka! We have made a discovery, an ethical guideline, albeit an implicit one.

One of the purposes of this motion is to bring these ethical considerations out into the open for rational discussion. We are putting the ethical questions on the map. In doing this we can get some useful insights from the ethical investment policy of the Church Commissioners and recent discussions on South Africa in General Synod. This brings us to at least three areas of major concern : British companies in South Africa, the defence industry and tobacco. I will begin with South Africa.

SOUTH AFRICA

South Africa is a country where political oppression goes hand in hand with economic exploitation. Black South Africans do not have the vote but they are a source of cheap labour. It is a profitable place for business and that is **the** reason why British companies remain there. Black wages are a small fraction of what whites earn. Health, housing and education all show similar levels of exploitation. The apartheid economy is intrinsically bound up with the large scale use of migrant labour and the consequent disruption of the normal patterns of family life.

Britain is by far the largest foreign investor in South Africa. There is no doubt that the current regime gains vital strategic and moral support from it. Apartheid could not survive without it. This has been increasingly recognised by the church in South Africa and black South Africans in general. A recent survey of black opinion in the townships revealed over 70% support for disinvestment. It is probably the last remaining non violent means of securing justice. The SACC are united in their call for such action. In July our own General Synod made a similar call and urged the Church's financial bodies to give a lead.

It is now too late to listen to the seductive voices telling us about the 'liberalising' influence of British companies in South Africa and stories of good works done in the name of advancement of black employees. Even if this were true — which it may be in some cases, but certainly is not in others — it is now too late. Black South Africans are in the apartheid prison. They are telling us, loud and clear, they are not interested in talk of refurbishing their cells. They want us to cut the bars and unlock the gates so they can be free.

By addressing appeal letters to major investors in South Africa we give credibility to their option to stay and continue as pillars of apartheid. And be in no doubt we **will** give them credibility : Barclays for example, produce a 16 page colour brochure about their giving; its all good PR and you need it if you are Barclays. We have to choose whether we are in solidarity with the shareholders of Barclays et al or the poor and oppressed black majority in South Africa, many of whom are our brothers and sisters in Christ. We have the choice. We can choose to stand in solidarity with the suffering portion of Christ's body in South Africa. I'm sure we will.

The motion lists the 'top ten' British companies : a list compiled by ELTSA. It includes those companies that are major investors and employers as well as those that are of particular strategic importance to the South African economy. It includes one of South Africa's major mining companies, Consolidated Goldfields which administers companies with nearly 100,000 employees. It includes BP Southern Africa — 100% owned by BP — which describes itself as 'one of the largest industrial concerns in South Africa'. RTZ — another mining company, made a total profit this year of £168M from its operations in Southern Africa, a quarter of the company's total profits. Other companies listed occupy strategic importance in the South African economy in oil, in that other lubricant of the economy, finance, and in producers of components essential to the industrial infrastructure.

But what is the link between ethical investment and ethical fundraising? If I may be allowed to state the obvious fundraising is not the same as investment! On the whole it is worse and in need of more careful monitoring from the ethical point of view as I will explain in a moment. But first and more importantly there is a simple moral connection between the two activities. When funds are withheld from a company on ethical grounds it is neither right nor reasonable to expect to reap the benefits of an investment we are not prepared to make. You cannot have your cake and eat it.

As well as this vital connection we must also remember that investment is different from fundraising, and the ethical implication of this. For example the Church Commissioners do have investments in companies with South African subsidiaries. They justify this in part by claiming it gives them the opportunity — as shareholders — to exert pressure to improve workplace conditions for black employees. And they can point to some successes. Clearly, asking for a donation does not enable such pressure to be exerted, since we are not all shareholders. From this example it is clear that fundraising criteria may need to be stricter than investment criteria. In general, investment criteria will provide a minimum baseline for fundraising guidelines to be developed.

The Church Commissioners guidelines represent a wide range of concern reflecting a broad consensus of Christian opinion. I will consider them in turn with reference to our appeal.

DEFENCE AND ARMAMENTS

I am not a pacifist so I accept the necessity of a defence and armaments industry. But I am deeply disturbed by some of that industry's business. Firstly its involvement in the arms trade. Sales of arms to the third world consistently and systematically distort the economies of the third world countries in an unacceptable way. It diverts much needed investment away from the provision of safe water supplies and food production. It causes the greatest misery — starvation, and disease amongst the poorest people. The arms bought are often used as the instruments of oppression by oppressive military dictatorships. We may need to keep down the unit costs of our own defence requirements but not at any price, and certainly not at **this** price. Secondly, the nuclear dimension of the industry is deeply troubling to the Christian conscience. In short, the defence industry cannot expect us to acquiesce in every proliferation and escalation of the appalling weapons it produces, and it cannot expect us to remain silent in the face of its greedy consumption of money and human ingenuity, resources which are both desperately needed elsewhere. British Aerospace is involved in the arms trade and nuclear capable systems. By going cap in hand to British Aerospace we shall not be able to raise these concerns with any degree of seriousness or integrity. By leaving them off our list we leave open the door for genuine and meaningful discussion. We have major questions to ask — it is important to ask them before we are bought off. The Church Commissioners do not invest in British Aerospace as a matter of principal. We should not for thirty pieces of silver undermine their decision by asking them for funds.

TOBACCO

The tobacco industry manufactures the deadliest product ever marketed. Do it yourself kits in packets of 20. Through coronary heart disease and lung cancer tobacco smoking accounts for 100,000 deaths each year in the UK. Out of every 1,000 young adults who smoke tobacco one will commit suicide, six will die in road accidents and 250 will die prematurely from tobacco. To put these figures into perspective, even in 1990 AIDS is **only** expected to be responsible for one tenth of this number of deaths. We have very good reasons for joining the Church Commissioners and omitting the Imperial Tobacco Ltd/Wills companies from our list.

ALCOHOL AND GAMBLING

My general coments on the Commissioners' criteria apply to alcohol and gambling and I simply draw your attention to the widespread problem of alcohol abuse. Although I think these areas are less important than the others I can see no good reason for our direct involvement in either area. The resultant undermining of the Church Commissioners stance here would surely be a backward step.

NEWSPAPERS

The exclusion of newspapers is not made on ethical grounds. The Church Commissioners in fact avoid investment in national newspapers on prudential grounds. All the nationals have a definite political line and in order to avoid accusations of bias they would have to invest in all or none. As all would include the Morning Star, I am sure they have chosen the wisest course. In Bristol we have only one local newspaper. So the question of taking sides with one paper against the line expressed in another does not arise. There is, therefore, no objection to an approach for funds being made from our **local** newspaper.

SLIPPERY SLOPES

At the end of the day we have to make decisions about individual companies. At this point we have to resist the temptation of allowing the complexities of the real world to beat us into submission. The drawing of guidelines is not easy, but that does not mean that no lines can be drawn or that no lines exist. In a rainbow the dividing line between say, blue and green maybe a little arbitrary. But we know that blue **is** a different colour from green. We know that we have crossed a line when we move from one to the other.

We need to remember this lesson in the ethical choices before us. There is no absolute and definitive point to draw our guidelines : the real world is resistant to such naive analysis. Despite these uncertainties real guidelines do exist as the analogy with the rainbow makes clear. We must locate them and apply them.

CONCLUSION

The proposal contained in this motion is one which takes into account the complexities of the real world. It recognises that it is not possible to peel off all the layers of our various involvements. But it also recognises the trap of allowing complexity to become an excuse for laziness. The motion may not be perfect, it certainly involves compromises and it could doubtless be improved. But it is still a sign of our ultimate concern with those values which transcend the merely material world of the market place.

REFLECTIONS ON BEING IN PRISON
Paul Baker

I have recently spent three days in Oxford prison. The sentence was a direct result of my refusal to pay a ten pound fine for 'obstructing the highway'. This was the charge brought against 152 people who took part in a blockade of USAF Daws Hill near High Wycombe, believed to be the control centre for cruise missiles deployed at Greenham Common.

The blockade was a symbolic act of resistance against our government's defence policy. Symbolic because it was planned to last for a limited period of time and because it involved only a small number of people. Any power it had to change the course of events had to come from the significance we attached to our actions and the meaning perceived in them by others. As a symbolic act of civil disobedience the action itself contained a mixture of co-operation and non co-operation with the authorities. For instance, most of us were willing to co-operate with the police as we were processed through the station at High Wycombe. But the action also had certain fixed points of non co-operation which were not negotiable. These varied from individual to individual. For myself there were three such moment: the initial decision to sit down in the road, the refusal to move when threatened with arrest for obstruction, and a willingness to go to prison if necessary. Looking back, with the advantage of hindsight, it seems to me now that of these three moments the spell in prison was the one which spoke most powerfully to 'outsiders'. What follows is an attempt to work out its meaning. By so doing I hope to answer the question I have been asked so frequently, 'Was it worth it?' Or as the prison officer put it just before my release, 'Was it good for the soul?'

I remember clearly the shock on the faces of policemen, prison officers and fellow convicts when they discovered my intended occupation. How could a future minister of religion — or any Christian for that matter — end up in prison? Surely, their faces spoke the words for them, being a Christian is about being good and respectable? Being in prison does not augur well on either count, so what kind of Christian are you?

In prison there is plenty of time to reflect! I remember thinking of some of the biblical heroes who spent time in prison and their reasons for being there: Jeremiah,

13

Peter, Paul and Silas, and from down the centuries many famous and not so famous names could be added. An impressive list to which you could add the name of Jesus who paid the highest price the law could exact. So what has happened to Christianity in this country to occasion such surprise when a Christian is jailed? Being a Christian has become too simplistically identified with being 'good' and being 'respectable'. Yet our founder rejected the epithet 'good' (Mark 10 v.18) and appeared to enjoy the company of unrespectable 'tax collectors and sinners'. Christianity has nothing to do with the sort of goodness which in reality is only a thin veneer of respectability. Our search for goodness and justice has to go deeper than this. Our calling is to stand alongside the oppressed and downtrodden and only then to work out the meaning of goodness and ask whether we live in a caring society. We have to remember Hiroshima and Nagasaki and find a way of expressing our solidarity with the present victims of the arms race in the third world and generations as yet unborn whose world we threaten to destroy.

This path of discipleship immediately undermines our claim to goodness and respectibility in the eyes of good and respectable people around us. Quite naturally we try and avoid it. Christians have been good at remembering they ought to visit those in prison. But they have erased from consciousness even the possibility of going there as inmates. The reason is not hard to find. You can visit those in prison whilst retaining and even increasing your standing and good character in the eyes of the world. But by being a prisoner you lose both. In so doing you and your guards have to ask all over again the real meaning of justice and goodness. And that is precisely the point of going to prison for the sake of conscience.

The prison officer asked me whether I had been 'in trouble' before. My immediate reaction was to reject the idea that I was in trouble at all. But in reality we were both in trouble in a world full to the brim with trouble. The superpowers are locked in a deadly embrace which threatens every living thing on this planet. For a thousand angry words and a thousand silences I bear my share of responsibility. By going to prison I do not claim any moral superiority for myself and still less to know all the answers. I had a more modest aim in view. By being in prison I hoped to write in graffiti red a big question mark on the walls of goodness and respectability that restrict our vision. I hoped to sow the seeds of a moral crisis which will bring about political change. The unbelieving look on the face of a prison officer when he realised why I was there convinced me, more strongly than any words, that my spell in prison was much more than just an empty gesture.

(First published in "Oxford Christians for Peace" Bulletin August 1984).

ORATION GIVEN AT PAUL BAKER'S FUNERAL ON MARCH 20TH 1989

Mick Fleming

I'm very glad to be able to say a few words about my friend Paul Baker, whose life we are celebrating today. The large and varied number of people here today, from all walks of life, and all shades of belief and opinion, are testimony to the way in which Paul entered so many people's lives from so many different perspectives and directions — and yet to everyone he remains just "Paul". In fact I don't think that Paul would be at all surprised at an atheist red speaking at the funeral of a christian green.

Paul was a man of apparent contradictions. A tireless fighter in the struggle for peace, justice and equality — yet a gentle and sensitive prop to so many of us. A Doctor of Physics — yet selfless in his efforts to explore the horrors of nuclear war. A man from comfortable circumstances — yet he devoted his life to the comfort and protection of the most vulnerable — not just in Knowle West but in Spitalfields too. A man for whom the doors of privilege were wide open — yet his was a life spent in opposition to the abuse of power and privilege — wherever it was to be found. A man of Christian belief — yet a man who chose to live the message of Jesus amongst those of other beliefs too, with the sacrifices which must accompany that road. A man who never knew hunger — yet campaigned for the starving. A man of great intellectual ability — yet spent time and effort enabling others to enjoy the freedoms of literacy. I said apparent contradictions — because of course they were not contradictions at all. They were the constituent parts of a man bound together by humour, humanity and principle.

I could list Paul's many achievements and activities — but I should simply like to say that he was my friend. I miss him, and I shall always remember with gratitude the life of a good man and the benefits for so many people which came from his selfless principled hard work, generated by his conscience and humanity.

Section Two

The first essay in this section tackles some of the issues and dilemmas inheret in being a prophet in the modern world. Paul Joyce considers the way in which prophecy has meant diffcrent things in different ages and the way in which it is vital to undcrstaiid some of the complexities involved in using biblical material to inform our own practice. His essay reflects upon the different meanings of the word prophet and the ways in which the prophets of the Old Testament interacted withiii their own contemporary social and political situation. He uses these reflections to offer some tools to help the modern prophet understand his or her role in contemporary society. The two essays which follow both tackle the issue of peace — a concern which was so central to Paul Baker's life and witness. Angela West uses two services held on Ash Wednesday 1984 at the Upper Heyford Air Base and on Hiroshima Day, 1988 as "remembering" events from which to develop her reflections. (See also comments in Gill Cox's Introduction and Sue Walrond-Skinner's essay). She considers the national need to remember the dead of two world wars and exposes the way in which the work of remembrance, if it were truly to be undertaken, without the comforting denials and glorification in which we indulge on cach Remembrance Sunday, would bring us face to face, not with the glory of our "glorious dead" but with the obscenity and futility of war. Her challenging critique links together our failure to understand the true consequences of war — for the poor, for the dispossessed, for the planet as a whole and she invites us to enter instead into a dialogue with the dead, whereby we become their witnesses.

The Gulf War took place two years after Paul's death and many of us felt the loss of Paul during that time as never before. We grieved for the loss of his leadership in the face of a compromised and collusive Church. Roger Ruston's essay focuses attention on the meaning of that war. He discusses the religious nature of war in general and the way in which for many people, the experience of war is the nearest they ever come to religious experience. This phenomena he argues helps us to explain the way in which the blood sacrifice of the soldier is identified with the supreme sacrifice of Christ and becomes therefore an event which cannot be questioned or halted without creating a kind of religious wrath. He suggests that the task of the Christian is to try to understand some of these compelling motivations and to engage in the effort to de-sacralise the facts and the interpretations of war.

PROPHECY AND THE MODERN WORLD
Paul Joyce

Many of those committed to the cause of justice and peace find within the pages of the Old Testament Prophets a major source of challenge and of encouragement. Moreover, the figure of the Old Testament Prophet, railing against the injustices of his day, provides a model for those courageous modern individuals and groups who are willing to risk life and reputation in the cause of challenging those forces which imprison and humiliate. There are indeed great riches within the pages of the prophetic books which can be a vital resource, and the idea of the 'prophet' and the 'prophetic' can express very important things in our own day. There are, however, a number of questions to be raised both about the use of the biblical books in this way, and indeed about the use of the words 'prophet' and 'prophetic' of modern critics of social and political injustice. We are not thinking here of problems which need worry only the cloistered academic; rather we are concerned to find ways in which these materials and these concepts can be used with integrity and with confidence, not least because careless use may place them at risk of being manipulated against the causes of justice and peace. How can the books of the Old Testament Prophets be used today with care and integrity, to encourage and facilitate renewed engagement with issue of justice and peace in ways appropriate to the end of the twentieth century?

'PROPHECY', ANCIENT AND MODERN

'Prophecy' has meant different things to different ages; indeed it can mean different things to different people living in the same period, as we shall see.

In ancient Israel itself there were several kinds of prophet; two broad types can be outlined here. They were not totally distinct, but were in many ways concerned with different things. There were the 'institutional prophets', based at the religious shrines or at the royal courts. They were paid officials, whose role was essentially to support the institution to which they were attached, providing religious legitimation for it. We find references to them in many of the historical books of the Old Testament (eg. 1 Kings 22.6). In sociological terms, they were 'central' figures, affirming the status quo and its values. Very different were the 'independent' or 'classical prophets', who from the time of Amos (about 760 B.C.) spoke a message of judgement against the nation as a whole and particular individuals within it. It is from these figures (or rather their disciples) that the prophetic books have come down to us. In sociological terms they are 'marginal' figures, challenging the values of the status quo (1).

It is, of course, the so-called 'classical prophets' who are of most relevance to our concerns here. It is important to be aware of the circumstances in which they worked. This is a matter of concern with any biblical material, but perhaps especially so in the case of the Prophets, for they were so much people of their day, addressing the challenging word of God to their own contemporaries. It is necessary to attend to the precise circumstances of their work, in so far as these can be known. We may sometimes be surprised — an example will illustrate how things may often prove less straightforward than we expect. Thus it is generally assumed that the classical prophets of the eighth centurey (Amos, Hosea, Isaiah and Micah) addressed a situation of relative affluence in which a wide gap had opened up between an increasingly leisured rich and a correspondingly downtrodden poor. It is commonplace today to draw parallels between this assumed situation and that of the industrialised West in our own day. There may well be some justification in such a parallel. However, the Dutch scholar de Geus has done valuable work on the social and economic background to the eighth century prophets, in which he argues that Israel and Judah had been in long-term decline and that this economic decline had borne most heavily on the poorer sections of society (2). If de Geus is right there might still be interesting parallels with our own situation, but they would be rather different ones from those which are commonly drawn. It is important to give attention to these matters, rather than simply assume that the context of the ancient prophets is self-evident.

We should be wary too about jumping to conclusions about what the Old Testament Prophets thought they were doing. We tend to assume that they were essentially moral teachers, that they were first and foremost concerned to call people to better behaviour. It may be argued, however, that the Old Testament Prophets were, in their own day, much less concerned with preaching repentance than we today tend to imagine. Though the call to repentance has a place, there is evidence to suggest that they were often more concerned with matters of 'theodicy', that is with the question of what God was doing in their day, how to explain and justify the ways of God. As the Assyrian or Babylonian Empire engulfed the Hebrew Kingdoms, the Prophets would tell their contemporaries: 'This political disaster is overcoming you because you have sinned against God's justice; it's probably too late to avert the disaster now, but at least you know now why this is all happening — you are being punished by God for your sins'. Such may have been the typical message of the Prophets in their own day, in a sense rather more negative and retrospective than we generally assume (3).

By the time of Jesus, it seems that ideas about Prophecy had developed in a distinctive way. Prophecy came to be thought of primarily in terms of the prophetic books which had by then achieved canonical status. The books of the Prophets were holy books which contained directions and predictions for the instruction of the reader. This perception also affected assessment of contemporary 'prophetic' phenomena, including the charismatic gift of prophecy, interpreted as one of the signs of the fulfilment of ancient promises. This represented a significant shift in emphasis. Whilst the element of prediction was not completely absent from the original work of the Prophets, this was not by any means at the centre of their concern — they cared much more about the present and what God was doing in the here and now. However, by the first century, the sense of the Prophets being men of their time addressing the issues of their day seems to have retreated almost completely. Their words had become Sacred Scripture, and they were naturally read in terms which spoke to the situation and needs of their readers (4).

But if understandings of Prophecy varied and developed in the ancient world, how much more if we bring the story up to our own day? For we live in a very different world from any of the bibilical cultures. A large gulf separates us (in our post-Marxist, post-Freudian situation) from the period in which the Bible was shaped. We must take the implications of this seriously; our reading of the Bible will inevitably be a fresh appropriation of an ancient text in a very different age. Many today use the word 'Hermeneutics' to describe the study of this process of interpretation; but often this only serves to mystify what is in fact a very natural feature of developing human culture. What meaning (or meanings) can the ancient text legitimately have in our day? This is a question which we must constantly address reflectively and self-critically.

In our own day the word 'prophecy' is understood in a range of ways. Let us briefly note just a few of the main uses. In popular parlance, it is most often used to mean simply 'prediction'. This is not totally unlike the notion current in New Testament times that the prophetic books contained predictions of the events of the reader's day. Another contemporary sense (indeed that which concerns us most here) is that of moral critique and challenge. This use is largely limited to church circles, and indeed to those of a liberal or radical persuasion. People will speak of Martin Luther King or Desmond Tutu as 'prophets', denouncing injustice in the name of God. This use is generally based closely on the model of the Old Testament Prophet, particularly as understood to be concerned primarily with issuing a call to repentance. Yet another sense of the word concerns Prophecy as a charismatic gift within the Church (which has an important place, of course, in the New Testament).

20

The political implications of this sense of the word 'prophecy' can sometimes be very different indeed from the sense of 'prophecy' as social and political critique. For example, in some areas of South Africa (and, of course, in certain other parts of the world), alongside groups in which the language of prophecy is used very much in terms of political critique, are to be found charismatic groups in which the language of prophecy is certainly used, but in a context which is often decidely apolitical in its orientation.

'Prophecy' thus has meant and can mean different things to different people, and it must be recognised that the word is applied to very diverse phenomena. We shall return later to questions of 'true' and 'false' prophecy, but we must acknowledge that actual usage is broad indeed. This should nor surprise us and nor should we attempt to limit the word artificially to any one meaning. Some uses of the term 'prophecy' in the modern world could be described as archaic, but then archaic terms and meanings frequently retain an important place in a culture, not least within sub-cultures (such as the Church) which are in part traditionalist by their very nature.

We today have the task of reapplying the biblical writings and images to make coherent and credible sense of them. Some of the likely original meanings will convey little to our times. Thus, if it is true that the original Old Testament Prophets were often more concerned with questions of 'theodicy' (e.g. explaining why the Assyrians were conquering Israel) than with a call to repentance, this is not likely as such to speak very directly to our situation, except by analogy. But then it would be a mistake to imagine that texts can have only one meaning, to assume that the original meaning (if it can be recovered) necessarily has absolute primacy in such a way as to rule out later uses of the material.

Obviously, common sense dictates that original meanings will be sought and respected, but we have to appropriate the material meaningfully within our own setting. Thus it may be entirely legitimate for us today to read the prophetic books as issuing a positive, prospective call to repentance, a challenge to bring about a just society, a better world. But let us remain thoughtfully aware that a process of interpretation is going on here, a reapplication of an ancient text to very different modern circumstances.

WAR AND NATURAL DISASTER AS INSTRUMENTS OF GOD'S WRATH

A specific illustration of the difficulties which can be involved in appropriating the books of the Prophets in a modern situation may be of help here: it concerns the implicit theology of God's judgement in history which underlies the Old Testament Prophets.

The question of how to handle the biblical theme of judgement today is a problematic one. Amos might be called the prophet of judgement **par excellence**: 'Prepare to meet your God, O Israel!' (4.12); 'Woe to you who desire the day of the LORD! ... It is darkness and not light' (5.18). The wrath of God is to be manifested in conquest and exile (presumably by the Assyrians, whose advance was still only in its early stages when Amos commenced his work (cf. 6.7, 14)) and is seen also in the earthquake which occurred near the start of Amos's ministry (cf. 1.1; 8.8; 9.5). Why does Amos proclaim his consistent message of judgement upon Israel? Several different rationales could underlie his tirade. Is it primarily that the flagrant sins which he observes demand punishment? Or is it rather that the international events and natural calamities which he witnesses or anticipates call for an explanation? Is it that he experiences a profound inner conviction that God is about to act? Or, again, could it be that his main concern is to encourage better behaviour in the future? These and other factors may all have a place. But what are **we** to make of the general theology of God's judgement in history which is implicit here, the basic assumption that God intervenes in world events to punish people?

This feature of Amos is found in many other books of the Bible. The basic theology of history we find here is shared by the other eighth century prophets who follow soon after him. A particularly striking example is found in Isaiah 10.5, where Israel's God declares, 'Ah, Assyria, the rod of my anger, the staff of my fury!'. There would seem also to be a close connection with the tradition which gave us the Book of Deuteronomy, which in turn underlies the great historical epic which stretches from the Book of Joshua to the Second Book of Kings. This long work of history tells the story of Israel from the Conquest of Canaan to the Exile, and presents it as a history of national sin which eventually meets its due divine punishment in defeat by Babylonia *(5)*.

But can we believe in a God who creates wars and causes earthquakes to punish his sinful people? Do we believe that God caused the Gulf War or Aids to punish people? The answer from a very few may be 'yes', but for most in the modern world the explanations for these phenomena are sought in the political and medical fields respectively. To be sure, we do not wish to say that God is absent from these situations — we struggle to relate them to notions of God's power and goodness. But do not some — many — situations resist theological interpretation? If the words of Jeremiah and Ezekiel seem plausible to us, as they explain the Babylonian crisis to be the result of the sins of the people, what of similar theological explanations when applied to Auschwitz or other horrors of our own century? We surely cannot indulge in 'double think', using one set of categories when watching the television news and another when in church or reading the Bible.

If something so fundamental as the underlying theology of history found in the prophetic books proves unacceptable (or at the very least highly problematic), can

22

we continue to read them as Scripture? Is not our continuity with the biblical witness in danger of being severed? Perhaps we need to find a way of 're-reading' the text if we are to appropriate it. If we feel that the book of Amos contains serious moral imperatives, that it speaks to matters which are of urgent ethical importance today, can we perhaps extract these challenges, whilst not 'buying the whole package'? We may wish to acknowledge that human dignity depends upon moral responsibility, and to affirm that justice matters to God — can we not learn these lessons from Amos without taking over his theology of God's judgement in history?

Or must it be 'all or nothing'? It may sound attractive to extract the moral, ethical lessons of Amos, whilst leaving behind his concept of God's judgement in the nation's history — but does this take seriously the integrated nature of Amos's theology? Is it possible to remove part of his message without distorting the remainder? Here we touch on a much broader issue, which we may describe as that of 'picking and choosing'.

'PICKING AND CHOOSING'

The prophetic books of the Old Testament contain much which appears to speak directly and powerfully to the needs of the modern world, much that the person committed to justice and peace will readily wish to cite. Isaiah 3.14-15 is typical of the passion with which the Prophets condemn injustice: 'The LORD enters into judgment with the elders and the princes of his people: "It is you who have devoured the vineyard, the spoil of the poor is in your houses. What do you mean by crushing my people, by grinding the face of the poor?" says the Lord GOD of hosts'. Corruption is exposed and denounced, and good news is promised to the poor: 'The LORD has anointed me to bring good tidings to the afflicted; he has sent me to bind up the brokenhearted, to proclaim liberty to the captives' (Isa. 61.1). There are powerful texts concerning peace too: 'They shall beat their swords into ploughshares, and their spears into pruning hooks; nation shall not lift up sword against nation, neither shall they learn war any more' (Isa. 2.4 (= Mic. 4.3); cf. Zech. 9.10). The Old Testament Prophets offer rich resources on other issues too, such as the place of the feminine (eg. Isa. 66.13, God is presented as saying, 'As one whom his mother comforts, so I will comfort you; you shall be comforted in Jerusalem'). Again, important things are said about creation and the natural environment, eg. Isa. 40.12ff: 'Who has measured the waters in the hollow of his hand and marked off the heavens with a span...?"

But there is other material in the Old Testament Prophets, which pulls in rather different directions from the texts we have just cited. The prophetic books occasionally reflect the perspectives of the powerful rather than the powerless — the book of Isaiah contains certain Royal and Zionist themes, and the book of Ezekiel certain Priestly themes, which tend to reflect (in part at least) the interests of the influential and the secure. Again, there is some material in the prophetic books which seems almost to glory in warfare and which certainly rejoices in the military overthrow of other nations (see, for example, the books of Nahum and Obadiah). Furthermore, there is much about women in the Prophets which is much less positive in its presentation of the feminine than the verse cited above, eg. Ezek. 16, 23; Zech. 5.7-8. Moreover, this is not merely a matter of certain books or strata taking a different line on particular issues. As we have seen, in some cases the elements which may be uncongenial to some modern readers (eg. the basic theology of history of the classical prophets) may well be all but inextricably interwoven with other themes which we may be keen to appropriate (such as the prophets' concern for social justice).

The Bible is indeed very diverse on most issues, and this is true of the books of the Prophets as much as of any other part of the canon. On what grounds might we legitimately stress one emphasis (eg. the concern for peace) rather than another? This is an important question, because the Bible can so easily be abused (as it was in support of National Socialism in Hitler's Germany and as it has been in defence of Apartheid by some in South Africa). If we are to discriminate within the diversity of the Bible, it is important that we do so self-critically, lest we encourage abuse of the text and play into the hands of those who would select for racist and other reasons. The South African theologian I. Mosala has shown how two communities in his country can both manipulate a shared body of texts in the interests of their own very different positions. He has argued that both Afrikaaner and Black theologians have frequently lacked a sufficiently sophisticated hermeneutic, and can sometimes in fact both be accused of abusing the biblical texts in rather similar ways (6).

Selection within the diversity of Scripture is certainly necessary. Whilst we must expose ourselves to the whole of Scripture and attempt to do justice to its full range, we must inevitably make judgements about what is more and what less central. The phrase 'picking and choosing' has, of course, a very pejorative ring to it, but something like this has been done (whether consciously or unconsciously) by readers of the Bible throughout the centuries (Consider, for example, the Protestant Reformers' elevation of the principle of Justification by Faith Alone). However, when we 'pick and choose' we must reflect carefully on what we are doing and why.

Some who favour liberationist readings of Scripture tend to assume too readily that the Bible naturally favours such readings, that it is self-evidently a book of the poor for the poor. But this runs the risk of being simply naive, for, as we have noted, there is much in the Bible, even in the prophetic books, which is not amenable to liberationist interpretation. A case needs to be made if it is to be claimed that the Bible demonstrates a bias to the poor. Rosemary Radford Ruether is one of those who have addressed this problem. The approach she favours is to highlight within the Bible a central theological thrust which is the key to the whole. She finds this in what she calls 'Prophetic Principles'. These, she says, 'imply a rejection of ... every use of God to justify social domination and subjection' *(7)*. Within the Old Testament she finds these principles in such material as the Exodus tradition and the sections of the classical prophets which focus on social justice. This strand of the biblical witness is given normative status, and all other elements in the Bible (including those passages in the prophetic books which represent different perspectives) are subjected to its critique. Ruether is absolutely right to make explicit the need to give normative importance to certain elements of the biblical witness, if we are to make sense of its diversity. However, even Ruether is too sanguine in her view that her 'Prophetic Principles' deserve the normative role she gives them. When she asserts that the 'prophetic-liberating tradition of Biblical faith ... can be fairly claimed, on the basis of generally accepted Biblical scholarship, to be the central tradition' *(8)*, she is surely underestimating the problematic nature of this question. She fails here to acknowledge the full range of ways in which the biblical materials have been used (and abused) and the need to *argue the case* for liberationist readings *(9)*.

On what **grounds** do we give certain parts and aspects of the Old Testament greater weight? In fact this question cannot be resolved without consideration of the broader context of interpretation. Christians naturally read the Old Testament in the light of the New. Can the New Testament then yield the key to our problem? Here we face the difficulty that the New Testament rarely speaks with one voice on any of the issues which are our concern here. There is not space to explore this now, but whilst many may claim rather confidently what is 'the message of the New Testament' on this issue or that, the reality is that such matters are rarely, if ever, as straightforward as they are presented. Not even the New Testament can, in its own right, give us unequivocal grounds for attributing greater authority to one emphasis rather than another within the Old Testament. Our principles of discrimination can be drawn only in part from within the Bible; we have to go outside Scripture too. It is interesting to note that Ruether in practice quite evidently draws upon a whole range of extra-biblical considerations when she chooses to give primacy to her 'Prophetic Principles'. This is in fact inevitable; we all tend to create our own 'canon' within the biblical canon, conditioned by our broader theological, confessional, ideological, and other perspectives. The important thing is that we should acknowledge that this is so. We must reflect honestly upon the issue of what non-biblical sources we draw upon — they might include, for example, Marxism, Feminism, Sociology, Psychology, and much else besides. How do we weigh the contributions from these non-biblical sources of insight? This leads on to yet bigger questions — how do we discern truth, indeed how do we know anything at all? In other words, what theories of epistemology and revelation are we working with? The range of questions raised can only be hinted at here, still less answered. But it is vital that we recognise that to attempt to draw upon the books of the Prophets in today's world is to commit oneself to engage — in one way or another — with all of these issues.

THE AUTHORITY OF THE PROPHETIC BOOKS

If the Bible is only one of a number of sources of authority (albeit a foundational one), how are we to characterise the place of the prophetic biblical resources and their authority?

Reading the Prophets might be described as listening to the witness of our older partners in faith, our predecessors who long ago wrestled with what it is to be human, in circumstances both similar to but also very different from our own. The Bible is not a magic box, full of blueprints for our life and faith in the modern world. 'Answers' to problems cannot simply be read off and applied to our own situations in a straightforward way. What we encounter in the pages of the Bible is the rich deposit of the story of God's people over a period of a thousand years or so, a mixed bag of profound insights and occasional blind alleys. We have here a wealth of models, analogies and hints, which can all play their part as the modern Christian engages in the complex and difficult business of reflecting upon the will of God in our day. If the biblical texts have an authority, it is an earned authority. It is not just because the Church tells us that these books are authoritative that we regard them as such. Rather, it is because they have proved themselves to be sources of wisdom, much as an old friend or a reliable guide is trusted — not infallible but generally trustworthy.

The prophetic books are a particularly rich source of such insight. However, they bring their own problems, for they are even less like a rule book than are some other parts of the Bible (such as the books of the Law). The style of the prophets is rhetorical, frequently dealing with issues **ad hoc** and **ad hominem**. The prophets are characterised by the fact that they address an urgent word to a specific situation at a particular point in time. This can occasionally make them seem rather elusive. Nevertheless, the fact that the prophets address particular concrete human situations does not necessarily mean that they are even more remote from us than they might otherwise be. On the contrary, this feature of specificity — 'down-to-earth reality', if you like — can actually be found to contribute to the power of the text, if the text is allowed to be itself (in all its otherness and strangeness), and not assimilated to our own very different situation too readily, in a facile or simplistic way.

Identity is a very important issue here too. The biblical books are the foundation documents of our tradition; they are an integral part of our continuity with the past, our identity in the present and our vocation for the future. Even if we part company with the biblical witnesses at certain points, we remain in respectful dialogue with them — or we run the risk of losing our Christian identity. We have seen that our continuity with the teaching of the Prophets (for example, on war as an instrument of God's wrath) can at times be stretched almost to breaking point. And indeed it may well be right, in particular cases, to lay aside significant elements of the teaching of the Old Testament Prophets. But we do not do so lightly. We retain the strong sense that these figures and their teaching hold vital clues to the purposes of God and our own integrity, that they are indispensable points of reference in our contemporary task of working for God's Kingdom in our world.

PROPHECY TODAY, TRUE AND FALSE

We have stressed the care that is needed in handling the prophetic literature of the Bible. Similar discernment is needed in assessing claims in our own day to speak a 'prophetic' word. When two individuals each claim to speak the word of God, how do we know whom to believe? This is an ancient conundrum, which we find within the pages of the Old Testament as the problem of 'true' and 'false' prophecy. The issue is a recurrent one in the book of Jeremiah, as in chapter 28, where Hananiah and Jeremiah, both described as prophets, confront one another, and each prefaces his speech with the words 'Thus says the LORD'. As the encounter is presented by the editors, we are left in no doubt as to who is the true prophet and who the false, but if we had been present in Jerusalem at the start of the sixth century B.C., to which would we have listened? This issue is very much with us today. In a stimulating recent article on this topic, Robert Carroll considers the claims of two British contemporaries to have heard the voice of God; the two people in question are James Anderton, the Chief Constable of Greater Manchester, and Peter Sutcliffe, otherwise known as the 'Yorkshire Ripper' *(10)*. These examples may seem rather far from the concerns of this essay, but how are we to weight the bold declarations of a Desmond Tutu or indeed an Ian Paisley?

Space does not allow for an extended discussion, but before ending this essay we may briefly note the contribution of a biblical book with a particular interest in prophets and prophecy, namely the Book of Deuteronomy. Deuteronomy offers not one but two tests of the true prophet. Deut. 18.21-22 may be considered first: 'And if you say in your heart, "How may we know the word which the LORD has not spoken?" — when a prophet speaks in the name of the LORD, if the word does not come to pass or come true, that is a word which the LORD has not spoken; the prophet has spoken it presumptuously, you need not be afraid of him'. This yardstick, of course, completely undermines prophecy as prediction, because if you have to wait and see if the promised event happens or not, you might as well not waste time listening to predictions at all! The other text is Deut. 13.1ff.; this is more directly relevant to our concerns and indeed even more thoroughgoing: 'If a prophet arises among you, or a dreamer of dreams, and gives you a sign or a wonder, and the sign or wonder which he tells you comes to pass, and if he says, "Let us go after other gods", which you have not known, "and let us serve them", you shall not listen to the words of that prophet or to that dreamer of dreams'. Note that in this case the requirement that the promised sign should come to pass is fulfilled and yet the prophet still 'fails the test' if he leads the people astray by false teaching. Prediction really is sidelined here. What matters is true teaching, or to put it more broadly, the whole life-style of the would-be prophet. We are reminded of the New Testament principle, 'By their fruits ye shall know them' (Matt. 7.16; cf. Luke 6.44. It is interesting to note that in its Matthaean form this saying is used precisely in relation to the problem of false prophecy). This may not be a bad rule of thumb for assessing such matters today. Does what is said build up the People of God? Does it foster tolerance, justice and peace? Does the declaration constitute an act of humility rather than of self-aggrandisement? These and similar questions will need to be asked, and we shall have to consider a broad range of evidence in making any such assessment. As argued above in relation to reading the prophetic books, such judgements will need to be set within the context of broadly-based theological reflection — and, of course, the very criteria we employ in judging 'fruits' will themselves have to be under constant scrutiny. A good pinch of scepticism is always appropriate in weighing claims to speak authoritatively in the name of God. And if this is true of the declarations of others, how much more will one have to be self-critical in assessing a call to speak a 'prophetic' word oneself!

Any reader who has persevered to this point might be forgiven for thinking that both the reading of the prophetic books of the Bible and the speaking of a 'prophetic' word for today are so beset with problems that neither is possible. We have all the more reason, then, to thank God that there are those who, taking their inspiration from the books of the Prophets (read with rigour and with self-critical integrity), have been ready to risk rejection and the threat of self-delusion to be prophets for our own times. One such was Paul Baker, in whose memory and honour this volume is published.

(1) For two rather different accounts of the relationship between 'institutional prophets' and 'classical prophets', see E.W. Heaton, *The Old Testament Prophets* (London, 1958; Revised edn, 1977) and J. Lindblom, *Prophecy in Ancient Israel* (Oxford, 1962). For a survey of sociological approaches to these matters, see R.R. Wilson, *Sociological Approaches to the Old Testament* (Philadelphia, 1984).

(2) J.K. de Geus, 'Die Gesellschaftskritik der Propheten und die Archäologie', *Zeitschrift des Deutschen Palästina-Vereins* 98 (1982), 50-57.

(3) For detailed discussion of this issue in relation to a specific Prophet, see my *Divine Initiative and Human Response in Ezekiel* (Sheffield, 1989).

(4) See J. Barton, *Oracles of God: Perceptions of Ancient Prophecy in Israel after Exile* (London, 1986).

(5) Lest any reader imagine that these are problems which can be confined entirely within the pages of the Old Testament, it should be pointed out that (whilst, of course, important differences are to be acknowledged) the Jesus of the Gospel tradition seems to share much with the Classical Prophets on the theme of divine judgement upon human sin.

(6) Cf. I.J. Mosala, *Biblical Hermeneutics and Black Theology in South Africa* (Grand Rapids, Michigan, 1989).

(7) R.R. Ruether, *Sexism and God-Talk: Towards a Feminist Theology* (London, 1983), 23; see also her 'Feminism and Patriarchal Religion: Principles of Ideological Critique of the Bible', in the *Journal for the Study of the Old Testament* 22 (1982), 54-66.

(8) R.R. Reuther, *Sexism and God-Talk*, 23-24. See also my 'Feminist Exegesis of the Old Testament: Some Critical Reflections', in J.M. Soskice (ed.), *After Eve: Women, Theology and the Christian Tradition* (London, 1990).

(9) For an important recent discussion of these issues, see C.C. Rowland and M. Corner, *Liberating Exegesis* (London, 1990).

(10) R.P. Carroll, 'From Amos to Anderton: Reflections on Being a Prophet', *Theology* 90 (1987), 256-263.

WHY REMEMBER THE DEAD?
Angela West

I didn't know Paul very well. I met him in the context of two events in the life of the peace movement. As I recall our participation in those events, I become aware that they contain essential clues about how to set about my task for this occasion. I find, as I write, that this reflection on the meaning of those events has become Paul's bequest to me — and others: a bequest of the dead to the living.

The first of these events was an Ash Wednesday service. This particular Ash Wednesday service was a bit different from others taking place that day in 1984; not so much in form — it was a fairly traditional liturgy — but in location. It took place beside the runway at the USAF base at Upper Heyford. Those present were ten members of a small Christian affinity group to which Paul and I belonged. Together with other such groups, we had been assembled by Christian CND at the base to link by our act of repentance this place and this day: a day of repentance at a place where our nation's defence forces maintain their readiness to deal out death to millions, if the word should come.

As our group stood chained together, shivering at the end of the runway, our prayers were drowned out every few minutes by the massive roar of engines from the F-111s, as they took off or returned from their exercise missions. Standing thus, beside out national defenders, it was not difficult to conjure up a consciousness of our morality. Old christian cliches like, 'The wages of sin is death' or 'The end of the world is nigh' leapt to life like outsize shadows from a torchlight on the walls behind. For an instant, death lost some of the abstractness it usually has for Westerners in good health and circumstances.

The second occasion I met Paul was at another service four years later. Here we recalled not so much our own deaths, and the deaths of those we intend by our national defence, but this time the dead from a particular event at the end of the second world war. It took place on August 6th 1945 — which, it so happens, is the Feast of the Transfiguration in the church's calendar. On this day, 43 years later in

Bristol's Catholic cathedral, a group of local people in the peace movement gathered to remember that day when the city of Hiroshima was 'transfigured' by a vast ball of fire dropping from heaven which turned its people into nothing but ashes and shadows. We remembered these dead by readings and prayers and by floating little candle lights on the waters of the baptismal font.

Afterwards I chatted to Paul over coffee. I hadn't seen him for several years. We renewed our affinity group bond so to speak, and spoke of people and concerns common to us. There was of course, nothing to forewarn me that this was the last time I would meet him, before he too was transfigured by death.

Thus it happens that the little I knew of Paul was somehow contained in these two remembering events. At the first, we were called by Christian tradition to 'remember' our death in relation to our sins. That death is both universal and personal we are no doubt already aware; but that it is also political and historical is perhaps less clear to us. The exact time and place and cause of my death is known only to God; but a competent statistician would be able to tell me the likelihood of it being from certain causes and not others. And the same information given to someone, say, from rural Guatemala would doubtless be very different. Of course, people go on dying in the same old way from the same old causes. They die from old age: but what age and whether this is 'old' will depend on which twentieth century society they come from; they die from disease; but which disease is similarly determined by social and economic factors. They may die from war; but the likelihood of this, and which weapons and which war caused death will have everything to do with the history and politics of their particular society. This may all seem like platitudes. But my point is this: as it is with death, so it may be also with sin. Those of us for whom sin is still a category relevant to modern living may nevertheless find that we are ill-equipped to confess our sins unless we understand more precisely what sort of sin we are implicated in. For people are not free-floating atoms, but rather cells in a body, of community, class or nation. And it is not just as individuals, but as members of these bodies that we are involved in sin. Thus, it is as a member of **this** society and **this** nation, and not another, that I am involved in the history of sin.

Those who gathered in the cathedral, on August 6th 1988 did so to commemorate the dropping of the atom bomb on Hiroshima and Nagasaki 1945. It is possible, I suppose, that they might have been there to celebrate the event which finally brought victory to the Allied cause in a war which the vast majority of people on that side regarded as a just war. But in fact our purpose was different. It was to express our deep regret and sorrow that so many unarmed civilians had been slaughtered without warning by means of this new weapon; and that such weapons of mass destruction had become the mainstay of the defence of the major powers in the post-war world. It was 'national sins' such as this which the members of our affinity group both recalled and wished to prevent when we made our repentance on the runway at Upper Heyford.

But those of us who gathered at Bristol on Hiroshima Day 1988 were not the perpetrators of the events we recalled. Some of us, including myself, were not even born at the time they took place. In fact, I was born a few months after the dropping of the first atomic bomb. Thus, at the time I was a classic 'innocent' civilian — an unborn child in my mother's womb. I shared this condition with those other unborn children whose mothers lived in Hiroshima and Nagasaki. Some of these never entered life at all, others did so, but grew up to find that they were under a curse. These were the *hibakusha* — those in whose bodies and offspring the poison of radiation might at any time manifest itself.

Meanwhile, I was born and grew up under no such curse it seems. If it is true that the 'sins of the fathers are visited on the children unto the third and fourth generation', it doesn't necessarily seem to be their own children that they are visited on. But perhaps we should not assume that the final reckoning for the events of the twentieth century has been completed. As an adult, I am no longer an 'innocent'. I inherit the results of my nation's history — and appropriate them. In my own case, I find I am drawn to discover more about this war in which my right to life and health was defended at such cost. What did it actually cost? And who paid? Should such a price ever have been paid? Is my inheritance in fact a series of debts?

To ask such questions about one's history is to embark on the work of remembrance. From the field of psycho-analysis, we are familiar with the idea that remembering can be, in some circumstances, a difficult and painful affair. Might it not be that searching the national memory is a similar kind of endeavour? Our annual November pieties for the 'glorious dead' do not seem to disturb us overmuch. Is that because there are questions we do not want to ask — and things we cannot afford to remember?

The bombing of Hiroshima was one of the concluding events of the second world war. And whereas some people now consider it an atrocity, there was at the time, and still is, a broad consensus that it was a regrettable necessity in a war that was basically meaningful and just. But as Paul Fussell shows in his book *Wartime*, to people at the time — especially those involved in fighting the war — things never seemed so clear cut as they do now. There was no spontaneous popular enthusiasm for the war, as there had been in 1914. Then people had joined up believing that this was the war to end wars, and found themselves involved in a protracted and senseless slaughter, in which almost a generation of young men was lost. Now, a quarter century later, it was happening again. As E.M. Forster said about the war in 1940, 'I don't want to lose it (but) I can't join in any build-a-new-world stuff. Once in a lifetime you can swallow that, but not twice'. Or as a Canadian soldier remarked, 'Who the hell dies for King and Country any more? That crap went out with the first world war'.[2]. The great gratitude shown by ordinary people to Neville Chamberlain at the time of Munich indicated the real enthusiasm for peace which existed at that time.

Traditionally, the just war is one in which the violence used to achieve the end is proportional to that end, which is one that primarily involves the defence and protection of the innocent. But as Fussell observes, even compared with the idiocies of Verdun and Gallipoli, the Second World War was indescribably cruel and insane. When the Allies invaded the continent, for instance, 1200 innocent French and Belgian citizens were killed because they happened to live in the wrong part of town, i.e. near the railway tracks.[3]. This was only one example of the frequent blunders and follies of this war, which world-wide killed more civilian men, women and children than soldiers, sailors and airmen. Not a great success, really in terms of the just war aim of protecting innocent civilians.

From the beginning there was an uncertainty about motives. For the troops, the war became like 'a bad job to be got through' so that they could go home and put behind them the embarrassment of not really believing in the cause they were fighting for, or worse — not even knowing what it was. This confusion about motives reached its climax when the Soviet Union, with Stalin at the helm, joined the crusade against totalitarianism, thus adding to everyone's embarrassment.

So if the troops had so little good reason for fighting, what in fact motivated them to fight at all? Most wars once started unleash a violence which has its own momentum, and the ancient motivation of revenge comes into play. For most US troops latterly, the war was about avenging themselves on the 'monsters' who bombed Pearl Harbour. They had little comprehension of Nazism, and were not aware of being part of a crusade to expose the extermination camps, or halt Hitler's drive to assert the domination of the Aryan race. In fact, they too were involved in a form of racial revenge themselves. Americans detested Japanese, who had had the affrontery to attack the US directly, killing US personnel and embarrassing US pretences to alertness and combat fitness. It was a 'sneak attack' by a people whom they regarded as little more than animals. Terms such as 'sub-humans' 'jackals' and 'monkey-men' were used by the US about the Japanese — all epithets that were paralleled by similar ones used by Germans to refer to Jews, Poles and assorted Slavs — and which were deemed to amply justify their vivisection. US servicemen collected Japanese skulls as souvenirs. 'Let's blast the Japs off the map' was a US slogan which by the end of the war had proved itself to be almost prophetic[4].

In popular remembrances, 'saving lives' is the official reason for Hiroshima. It must be all of a piece with the war myth that serves to keep us clean. Other motives must be repressed from recollection — for they do not form part of the picture we have of ourselves. Thus we do *not* remember how the bombing of Hiroshima was part of the US race to gain military and technological superiority over its rival the USSR; and how it offered a convenient opportunity for testing a new weapon and at the same time paying off an old score against a racially despised enemy. Even those who now think of Hiroshima as an atrocity may, it seems, be capable of a bit of selective forgetting:

> 'I distrust people who speak of the (atom) bombings today as an atrocity they strongly opposed in 1945... I don't believe them. At that time, virtually everyone was delighted that we dropped the bombs, not only because they shortened the war and saved thousands of American lives but also... because the 'Japs' deserved it for the terrible things they had done to our boys at Pearl Harbour, Bataan, Guadalcanal, and all the way through the Pacific'.

Thus the motives that do not square with a national self-image of decency and fairness are quick to drop out of memory. Also lost to remembrance is much of the unpleasant reality of the war itself. In the UK, we remember with fond nostalgia the civilian togetherness during the blitz; but we do not remember the corpse robbers who operated so skillfully in these conditions. We do not hark upon the bitter anti-Jewish graffiti that appeared on the walls of bombed out buildings. In retrospect, we might concede that those in concentration camps experienced war as hell. But this is somehow seen as an aberration in a war which elsewhere was cleanly and decently fought — at least on our side — and which we still obsessively re-live in popular film and fiction. Only a minority of troops were engaged in frontline combat, and came to know from first-hand that war is hell, an organised insanity. But these have not been allowed to disturb the rosy picture of national heroics with their nightmares of murderous carnage and dismembered bodies.[5]

This war then, in which my right to life was defended at such cost, was not really a Good and Just War as it is now seen, but just a war like any other war — stupid and sadistic, one in which, according to Dwight MacDonald 'the maximum of physical devastation accompanied the minimum of human meaning'[6]. Thus, the work of remembrance, the effort truly to remember our dead, brings us face to face not with the glory of our glorious dead, but with the obscenity and futility of their deaths. It becomes clear that the last war has indeed laid the foundations for the society in which we live — but not quite in the manner that it has been presented to us. Despite our annual pieties in the direction of the war dead, as a consumer society, in which the common good is the consumption of goods and services, we really have no use for the dead. Once their last act of consumption (the funeral) is over, it doesn't matter much any more what they fought for, whose side they were on. The consumers are consumed, they become dust and ashes — mere waste matter. This is a break from most other societies in history, where in a sense, the dead continue to have their place among the living.

It is only recently that our dialogue with the dead has begun to fall silent. In past ages, people could not afford to forget the dead, because they saw their fate as intimately linked with that of the living. In Christendom, this relation was expressed by the anticipation of the Last Judgement — the coming of a final righting of injustice, the punishment of the guilty and the rewarding of the innocent. This was a feared and fearful mystery that the dead had been initiated into, and the living were still uncertain of its implications for them. The story of Dives and Lazarus in the gospel works with this imagery, while reminding us that the dead are not able to bring back warning from another world. While the possibility of this other world was still vivid in popular belief, there was no escape from the task of preserving the memory of the dead, attempting to assess their lives so as to bring guidance to those who would one day follow them.

But what has become of this powerful imagery that for so long conditioned the European religious and popular imagination? Who gives it a thought these days? Has it really vanished without trace — faded away in our changed social and political conditions? Perhaps on closer inspection, we may find that it has not so much been forgotten as been realised — that is, anticipated by us in our social, economic and political arrangements. Thus, in our present world there are the few who are saved — saved from the pangs of hunger, thirst and want, they feast daily at the 'heavenly banquet' a food supply of such abundnce and variety that earlier ages could scarcely have imagined it; and there are the many who do not feast but starve, the many who are consigned to the outer darkness of poverty and the hellish flames of war.

But we, who are among the saved — how do we know that we are saved? We know because we see that in us the promises of scripture are fulfilled. Do we not have life in abundance as promised — here in the consumer paradise where our only duty is to sing the praises of that which sustains us in a never ending pattern of consumption? Have we not become 'children of light' — here in the well-lit world of our homes, our shopping malls, our places of worship and public entertainment — where the fantastic play of light is everywhere apparent? Are we not safe and secure from our enemies — and the hands of all who would rob us of our goods? And if not 100% secure from accident and theft, at least well-insured. In this our 'paradigm of heaven' there are only the living — all memory of the dead is absent. The temples of consumption, our supermarkets and shopping precincts give no house-room to the dead whose ancient sites they often stand upon. For in heaven, history comes to an end. As we come into our inheritance, we no longer need the intercession of the saints. Here there is no past and no future — only an eternal present, where we have become like the angels ascending and descending on Jacob's ladder — but now it is on the escalator of the department store, like Debenhams in Bristol on a winter evening, where 'angels' can be seen from the street swathed in light, ascending to the seventh floor. At that time of year when the church's calendar bids us remember the dead at the feasts of All Souls and All Saints, we are just about to embark upon that great annual national binge of the winter solstice, when the advertisers urge us on to ever greater heights of 'Christmas giving' — so that everyone will continue to receive what they are accustomed to, and our paradise continue.

And what of those who are damned by their poverty from offering the praise of continual consumption? They must not be allowed to enter the light, but must remain well hidden from the sight of the elect. Their place is the place of shadows, close to the dead and the land of Sheol.

Thus we have represented the Last Judgement on earth. We have used all our scientific and technical ingenuity to find a 'final solution' to the threat of God's justice. For in the Twentieth Century we know ourselves to be image-makers on a grand scale: the whole world has become a theatre for our cosmic dramas and their special effects. At the press of a button whole populations can vanish; the unearthly glory of the Transfiguration is ours to perform. Why then should we wait on God — who by all accounts is notoriously unreliable — to act in such an important matter as the final judgement when we have all the means available to do it ourselves? Surely we, who in the Gulag and the extermination camps, have perfected the construction of hell, can be relied on to design a heaven for the elect?

Unfortunately for us, there are traitors in our midst, most intimately present in fact, and ever-ready to undermine our designer paradise. These are the 'enemy within' or rather, should we say, the enemy within which we find ourselves confined, that is our bodies. In 'Pilgrim's Progress' there is a conversation in which Hopeful tells his friend Christian how he first came to look after the good of his soul. When he became convinced of his sins, it gave him 'such heart-affrighting hours that I couldn't bear, no, not so much the remembrance of them upon my heart'. Sometimes he managed to get rid of this troublesome remembrance, and to carry on enjoying the good things of life in Vanity Fair and avoid being 'shaken with the Word'. But then his 'convictions' would return and he would be 'as bad, nay worse, than before' Christian asks him. 'Why, what was it that brought your sins to mind again?' Hopeful replies that there were many things, and one of them was 'If mine head did begin to ache...'[7]

Who would have thought that the simple headache could be such a traitor? Of course, that was the seventeenth century, and now we have Panadol, and modern medicine and private health care. But the headache remains, and so do many of the aches and pains of ageing; and as long as they are around we shall never quite be able to forget that death, though it may have been postponed, has not been eliminated and slowly tightens its grip through the now extended period of our ageing. Those who are saved, it seems, are not saved from this. Our youth and energy we took for granted — used it as lightly as advertisers' 'free gifts' believing that there was plenty more where that came from. But now, suddenly we find that it is not everlasting, it can be used up, leaving us a prey to dangerous memories. We may become 'vulnerable' to the memory of those whose youth was used up before it had hardly begun — the abused children, the children of the malnourished and exploited. Or perhaps we remember those who were 'used up' in the processes of modern war — the young soldiers slaughtered on the field, the civilians young and old, male and female slaughtered in and around their homes, and the victims of nuclear radiation. Like latter-day King Lears, perhaps the exposure to our own infirmity will bring us to the realisation of theirs; 'Ah, I have ta'en too little care of this'. As memory continues along these dangerous paths we may become aware that it is not only modern war that 'uses up' people but the whole structure of modern production as it ceaselessly supplies the 'heavenly banqueting table' of the consumer paradise. Of course, the authors of paradise have never been too dismayed by this using up of people, because, as everyone knows, people is what we are reproducing all the time — there is certainly no shortage of people. But nowadays there begin to be nagging doubts. For like the youth that we falsely take for granted, there were other 'free gifts' that we received without question, never doubting their availability when needed. In our reckless proceeding, we never noticed until now that the burden of inflated consumption, the endless abundance and the brightness which abolishes the nightime has its cost. A huge unpaid bill awaits us. Nature herself is not infinite. We find we have strained and depleted all her resources up to breaking point. We have begun to poison the sources of our life, air, earth and water with the products of our excess. This is a headache for which there is no Panadol.

In response to this crisis, we try desperately to purify and privatize — to operate the time-hallowed practice of ensuring that the 'fittest' — those who already have the most resources — continue to have greatest access to what is left. These limited resources now include clean air, clean water, and unpolluted earth. For the poor, the people of the shadowlands, these things have not been 'free' for a long time now. But we, the elect, believed until recently that such things were supplied free of charge by Nature. Now it seems, she has withdrawn her services. Who is this, we begin to wonder, that has the power to threaten us with want? Newly impressed with her power, we re-enthrone Nature as our new-but-ancient Goddess. She is a re-incarnation of the virgin-mother, pure in herself but abundantly fertile — or so we thought. We seek to placate her in all things (100% natural ingredients, natural childbirth etc). And for a little while, wrapt up in our new devotion, we manage to exclude from memory the fact that this same Goddess who brings life, also brings death — death in childbirth, as well as in old age, natural and 'unnatural' death for young and old through flood or fire, earthquake, disease or accident. Nature is as generous with death as she is with life — and 'eternal' life is not in her gift. She is in fact, another idol as false as the deity we invoke to bless our battleships, and wage war on our side. Nature, arrogated to the role of Goddess, is as merciless as war.

Thus, nature and living with our biorhythms, is ultimately powerless to stave off the memory of mortality which returns to us with the headaches and all the other aches which presage our final destiny. This memory, which we were required to leave at the gate of paradise, has managed to climb over the fence; we remember painfully what it was so much more convenient to forget. We cannot help remembering what is the element missing from our version of the Last Judgement. It is of course, justice, the reward of the innocent and the recompense of the wrong-doers. We had replaced it with the arbitrary election of the few to a life of abundance, and the arbitrary damnation of the many to a half-life in the shadowlands. We have been led to believe that we were the just because we inherited what was due to the just; and those who were still perversely preoccupied with feelings of guilt were offered therapy for their problem. But now we are forced to remember that we are not the just — only the lucky. We have divided the world into the lucky and the unlucky and reinforced the division. We have tried to imitate what we could not deliver — that is, judgement. But it is a failure. Our 'judgement' is neither final nor just. It can hasten death for some and postpone it for others — but it can deliver no-one from death. It seems that after all, we may have to look to God for judgement. We shall have to wait on God, hoping or fearing but knowing nothing for certain, making do with promises. Reluntantly we remember that history and sin have not been abolished, and therefore we are not free from questions of guilt and responsibility, such as we began with. We are obliged to wrestle with the whole question of where we belong in the history of sin.

Thus, the question presents itself to me: am I, the innocent who was 'protected' by the bombing of Hiroshima, still innocent? Can I, as adult, continue to be innocent of the means by which I am defended? I think not. Yet, I do not know how I can elect a just defence. I do not know, in fact I am afraid to know what exactly it would mean for me to prepare myself for the coming of justice. I cannot be certain that justice will come — only of death am I certain — and of the uncertainty of death. How many Dives are there now on that other side who currently petition God to be allowed to bring warning to such as me? The death of someone close to us is painful. But what if on that other side we encounter closely not first of all those who were close to use in life but those who were, as it were, close to us in death — our victims, or those who were sacrificed on our behalf? Wilfred Owen, in his poem, *'Strange Meeting',* imagines that he escapes from the battle to a place where:

> ...encumbered sleepers groaned,
> Too fast in thought or death to be bestirred,
> Then as I probed them, one sprang up, and stared
> With piteous recognition in fixed eyes,
> Lifting distressful hands, as if to bless.
> And by his smile, I knew that sullen hall —
> By his dead smile I knew we stood in hell.

The one who recognizes him is in fact, the enemy he killed, who, when he implies that perhaps Hell is not so terrible after all, reminds him of:

...the undone years,
the hopelessness, Whatever hope is yours
Was my life also... I am the enemy you killed, my friend.

Shall I expect to meet those Japanese contemporaries of mine, formed in the womb as I was, yet who did not enter life as I did? For my government, in its wisdom, had decreed that for my protection, they should not be allowed to live.

Thus, I begin to seek out dialogue with the dead, and begin to experience myself, not as one of the living whose life is self-evidently justified, but rather as a survivor. And as a survivor I must face up to some hard questions such as: why were they forced to die and I permitted to live? In what ways am I more deserving of life than they? If I am honest I must admit that there are none. What then is the purpose of my life? How can it be justified in relation to their deaths? I do not know. But can it be that these deaths oblige me to be their witnesses? Is it up to me to ensure that their story is told, the story of what they suffered and how they died? Must I try to set the record straight so that other survivors can judge rightly and look to their own lives and action? Is this the way to prepare for the 'final judgement'?

One of the great 'witnesses for the dead' of our times is Primo Levi, survivor of Auschwitz and it is he who writes with profound lucidity of the painful ambiguity of the role of survivor. He writes of the sense of shame experienced by survivors [8]. Though knowing that he is not guilty of a crime, the survivor is prey to the suspicion that 'everyone is his brother's Cain' and is aware that he is alive in the place of another — one who may be more sensitive, generous, wise, or otherwise more worthy of living than he. In the context of his holocaust experience this perception is the more acute. He describes how after his return from imprisonment, he was visited by a religious friend of his, who suggested to him that his survival was perhaps not mere chance, but the work of Providence. He was a person touched by grace, a 'saved' man. But 'why just I?' asks Levi. The friend suggests that perhaps it was because he had to write and bear witness.

But Levi rejects this as 'a monstrous opinion' which could serve only to aggravate the shame of the survivor. For, as he says, the 'saved' of the Lager were not the best, those predestined to do good, to bear a message. His experience suggested the contrary — that it was rather the selfishly violent, those who had conquered a position of privilege, the collaborators and spies who were most likely to survive. The 'fittest' — that is the worst — managed to stay alive; the best all died.

He does not however, reject totally the idea of witnessing for the dead. He says he has done so as best he could, and will continue to do so whenever the opportunity presents itself. Then he says, 'and I also could not have done so.' For what he rejects completely is the idea that his testifying could by itself gain for him the privilege of surviving when so many had died. For him there is no proportion between the privilege and its outcome. 'We the survivors', he says 'are not the true witnesses. We are an anomalous minority those who by their prevarications, abilities or good luck did not touch bottom. Those who did, did not return to talk about it.' These — the drowned or submerged — are the complete witnesses, the only ones whose deposition would have a general significance.

Some of us, after a close inspection of the cruel canvas of our history, may feel that the only role that makes sense for us to adopt is that of witness for the dead. If this is our case, then we must first acquaint ourselves with the sobering reflections of someone like Primo Levi who has passed closer to the heart of darkness of the twentieth century than we are ever likely to. If we are believers, then we must also face fully the fact that Levi is not a believer, and declares that after the season of Auschwitz he is even less of one. Thus, what this witness has to report cannot serve to shore up our faith. On the contrary, it may deeply disturb and unsettle the comforting nostrums that have become part of our religious inheritance.

'He died that we might live' we are accustomed to tell ourselves: and shaken by the loss of sons and brothers in two world wars, we use it as a comforting cover-up for the gash in our sense of a well-ordered universe produced by these deaths. We seek to restore order and meaning by means of a suitable epitaph. But let us pause to ask: Why did 'he' have to die that we might live? Have we stopped to consider what a barbaric idea we are endorsing. Who was he, in what circumstances did he die, and by what reckoning do we deem it 'necessary' that he should die so that we might live?

To take seriously the testimony of those who have been to the edge of the abyss and returned means that our faith cannot remain untouched. We are sent back to scripture with hard questions. It may be that we decide that the 'answers' are inadequate to the experience of the victims of the Twentieth Century holocausts, even derisory and insulting. Or it may be that we discover to our shock that there are no 'answers' as we once thought. Not only are there no answers in this sense, but we see perhaps that up till now we have never really understood the question. If we do not lose faith entirely in this encounter, it may be that our faith will become a new understanding of scripture as an arena of discourse available to 'survivors'. The question identified as essential by the theologians of the holocaust is one that the New Testament also addresses. In fact, it speaks rather more directly to this question than many of those other questions to which we have formerly found answers in it. The question is this: whether or not the persecutors will at last triumph over their victims. In the New Testament this concern finds expression in the question of whether death has the final victory. It is the question about whether this history of sin, which we the living have shared with the dead, will one day be brought to final judgment.

If this comes to pass, as Christians believe, then what will be the situation of those of us who, while living in the midst of the most cumulatively violent society of all in world history, have nevertheless been, whether they like it or not, the protected beneficiaries of that violence? We proclaim a god of justice and mercy. But wouldn't such a God, who brings true judgment, first reward the innocent who suffered violence and death? And why should we suppose we are first in line for mercy when there are all the millions who received no mercy in this life? What then have we to expect from judgment, we who have already received our reward in the protection we have enjoyed during our lives?

Thus, to believe in the Resurrection after this encounter may mean something very different from what it meant before. It may mean that we understand it not as an event that is unchangeable by subsequent history, but an event that, so long as history is still in process, is still vulnerable to history. Thus, like a child who is born full of promise but later dies through starvation and neglect, the resurrection may be a sign of hope that is capable of reversal, so long as history has not had its final outcome. Perhaps the worst of all possible 'final judgments' would be to be left forever with the judgment we have made ourselves. Yes, even for those like us who, on the face of it, stand to lose in God's final judgment.

What then can believing in the Resurrection mean for us? It can mean that we express our hope for the coming of justice — for the dead as well as for the living. But we do not yet know whether the dead are raised. And it is as St. Paul warns: 'If the dead are not raised, then Christ has not been raised either. And if Christ has not been raised, your faith is futile; you are still in your sins. (I.Cor.15.16).

So faced with this potential futility, there are two choices we can make. Either we can give up and go home. For after all home is quite comfortable and we may as well enjoy it while we can and forget about sin and all that stuff. The other option is less reassuring. We can choose to accept the promise of Scripture concerning the Resurrection — absurd, shaky and increasingly uncertain as it seems, we can proclaim our hope that justice will be done — even if that doing of justice may be our own undoing. For we know now that we, the elect in this life, are by no means justified nor can we still pretend that we are innocent. So why then should we opt for that which threatens to convict us? It may be that, perversely we find that we are unable to be convinced by any other truth about the world that is currently on offer. And so our 'conviction' remains. Or it may be that we find ourselves unable to give up on the dead. We cannot escape the sense we have that we are still 'one body' with them. Death does not manage to sever completely the family bonds with these our sisters and brothers like Paul who have gone before. It is this sense of continuing community with our dead, and our dependence on them that the Church recognizes and claims for her own when she speaks of the Community of Saints. When such as Paul have left us for the other side, we want to affirm that he is still with us and we with him in the work that we share. And so we are confirmed into, or perhaps lured into, a belief that death is not the end. Thereby we become committed to a role for which we are not sure we have the necessary courage and understanding to undertake. It commits us to becoming witnesses for those dead who have been exposed to violence and injustice in this life. It falls to us to plead their case at the bar of history. And it generates in us the hope, with or without cause, that they will one day plead for us before the Mercy-Seat of God.

1. Paul Fussell, *Wartime, Understanding and Behaviour in the Second World War,* OUP 1989.

2. ibid. p.131

3. ibid. p.283

4. ibid. p.117

5. A compiler of *An Oral History of the War Years in America.* See Fussell p.283. n.43

6. ibid. p.143

7. John Bunyan, *The Pilgrim's Progress* Penguin Classics p.189-90

8. Primo Levi, *The Drowned and the Saved,* Abacus 1988. See especially Chap.3 'Shame'

THE WAR OF RELIGIONS AND THE RELIGION OF WAR

Roger Ruston O.P.

If there is going to be a 'new world order' after the collapse of Communism and the end of the bipolar world of the Cold War, it is not going to be born without dangerous conflicts and chronic disorders for large numbers of people. At the centre of many of the conflicts, providing an aggravating force — if not the primary motivation — will be religion. Obviously not all religiously mixed areas of the world are heading for disaster, but those in which difference of religion is allied to long-standing inequalities of power between ethnic and cultural groups are the places where conflict is most likely to occur in the near future. Northern Ireland turns out to be not merely an odd corner of Europe somehow stuck in the quarrels of the seventeenth Century, but a very persistent example of something more widespread. Combine this with the resurgence of anti-semitism in almost every European country (to say nothing of Arab ones) and with the massive unfinished business between Islam and the Christian West, and we have an alarming picture of the possibilities for religious wars ahead of us.

However, I believe it would be wrong to conclude that religious wars are somehow different from other wars, either in their motivation or their ferocity, or that a world without religions would somehow be less liable to war. The association of religion with war goes deeper than differences of cult. In an important sense war simply *is* a religious phenomenon, which readily feeds on the symbols of existing religions.

In modern times, the debate about war — even when it takes place between christians of different opinions — appears to be conducted most often on the level of morality, as something we ought or ought not to be involved in from the point of view of the moral virtues, notably courage and justice. Those christians who think that war is sometimes a duty, argue each particular case on the grounds of justice: a just cause may not be sufficient to justify action, if other criteria are not satisfied, especially discrimination and proportionality in the fighting. Even those christians

43

wholly opposed to war often appear to base their case on an idealist morality which they attribute to the teaching of Jesus: the morality of non-violence, a New Testament *thou shalt not.*

However, I believe that purely moral considerations never get to the heart of the matter. They cannot, for instance account for the near-universal opposition to war among the early christians and the manner in which this was expressed. But most seriously, they cannot account for the kind of extreme emotions which people experience in time of war and the type of contestation which very quickly overtakes the calm debate about justice and prospects for future peace once the fighting has begun. I wish to argue that war is always a deeply religious phenomenon; that this has become manifest in the twentieth century; that christian approaches to it should begin from the understanding that it is a religious phenomenon; and finally that this is the most serious grounds for christian opposition to it.

THE RELIGION OF WAR

We have recently been involved in an international war in which religious talk was very much on the surface, on both sides. It began with the political and military leaders, who tried to make it clear — perhaps to God in the first place, and the rest of the world afterwards — that their cause was God's cause. This early resort to God is partly due to the fear which human beings who are supposed to be in control of events experience when they are facing a situation which they cannot control. The religious anxieties which people have in war is a sign that their easy peace-time relationship with the divine is under strain. War reveals that they do not have the kind of control over the outcome of events which they take for granted when things are going well. The rusty old disused machinery of prayer gets a kick in the hope that it is still connected. While the outcome remains uncertain and so much depends upon it, including perhaps their own survival, even political leaders become men of prayer for a time. Their prayer is addressed to what the Bible calls the 'God of Battles'. And it is calculated to exite those religious emotions among the population without which it could not be mobilized for the sacrifices ahead.

It is easy to believe that the religious language of leaders is aimed at public opinion rather than at God and that there is some kind of manipulation of base religious emotions going on. However, to dismiss it that easily would be a serious mistake of understanding. It would fail to take seriously the genuine religious content of the situation. In biblical terms this religious content is known as *idolatry*: the worship of a god different from the God of the Covenant — a something in the world with whom the transcendent God is easily confused when people's deepest worldly interests are involved. Those who use religious language in these circumstances are making the claim that their deepest interests coincide with those of God and his righteousness, and that consequently the most serious of absolutes is at stake and that they have a sacred duty to see that it is upheld.

By the time we were two weeks into the Gulf war during January 1991, the air was as thick with religious language as it was with missiles. When President Bush said 'We *know* that this is a just war. And we know that, God willing, this is a war we will win', he was using the common currency of religious language, more than matched on the other side by Saddam Hussein.[1]. Of course the American leaders of the coalition were careful to avoid any suggestion that difference of religion entered into the Gulf war in any way. How could they? Being Christian or Muslim was not the issue. The quasi-religion of sovereign states was the issue. The integrity of sovereign state borders is a kind of absolute of the modern world order. It is that which allows politicans to excite the popular religious passions which are necessary for going to war. In conflicts where existing sovereignty is not clearly and blatantly violated by outside powers, as in East Timor, Mozambique, Tibet or the Kurdish lands, no amount of injustice and slaughter of the innocent can motivate the great powers to intervene with a 'just war' on behalf of the victims. The cardinal sin — the only thing the United Nations can sanction a war for — is aggression against a sovereign member state.

It has been widely argued that the violation of Kuwait's sovereignty by Iraq was the pretext rather than the ultimate cause of the intervention; that access to oil was the deciding factor, and that the whole elaborate pretence of UN resolutions and solemn recital of Just War doctrines was a moral fig leaf for purely material interests. As was said at the time by an American official, if Kuwait produced carrots instead of oil there would have been no anti-Iraq coalition and no war. But an association of material interests with religious passions is nothing new in the history of armed conflict. They do not exclude one another. Indeed, religion may be at root an elaborate mechanism for coping with rivalry over material interests within communities.[2] By suppressing rivalry and violence within communities it serves to united them against outsiders who threaten the interests of the community as a whole. And nothing unites them so closely as blood sacrifice. The sacrifice of young men on the battlefield is the critical event which seals the unity of the community and the justice of the cause, allowing the identification to be made with God's justice.

The Great War of 1914-18 was the time when this identification was most evident and most of our military-religious symbolism — such as that of Remembrance Day — is a product of that cataclysm.[3] In some ways the Great War was a kind of revelation — in the way the Crucifixion was a revelation — of humanity's true condition. Sentiments were voiced with a kind of naivety and innocence which today British people at least would be very wary of, even though the feelings are still there. It was then that the parallel was widely made between the sacrifice of soldiers at the front and the sacrifice of Christ. The words commonly carved on the war memorials on village greens all around our country are, *"They died that we might live"*: deliberately associating the deaths of young warriors with the sacrificial death of

Christ. In the Great War, and to a lesser extent in the wars which have followed, there was a deep confusion between the goals of the nation at war and the purposes of God; between economic self interest and justice. There was a deep confusion between Christ's willing submission to the violence of others on the Cross and the deaths of soldiers bravely doing their job killing others; between prayer for victory and the christian prayer 'thy will be done'; between the solidarity demanded by the nation-state and the solidarity of love which is required by the kingdom of God.

Despite the passage of years and the steep decline in religious observance, there were strong echoes of this mentality during the Gulf War. Once the fighting had begun in January 1991, religious words and emotions connected with the supreme value of blood sacrifice in the defence of the principle of sovereign statehood were again widely apparent. Memories of Appeasement and the failure of the Western powers to resist Hitler were reactivated. Rational discussion of the issues become impossible once the forces were committed to the retaking of Kuwait and blood began to be spilt and religious emotions engaged. At an early stage of the Gulf war, on the Western side, dead soldiers were described as fallen warriors who perform, like Christ, the 'ultimate moral act'. The use of this imagery is explained by the fact that for many, even non-churchgoers, christianity provides the only language available with which to express the religious absolutes which the reality of war evokes. In Arab countries a parallel, but more confident, language of sacrifice was used on both sides of the conflict. Both Christianity and Islam lend themselves perfectly to the task set by the religious nature of war.

Indeed, for many people, war is the nearest they ever come to religious experience. There is a special wrath reserved for those who seem to suggest, by calling for an early halt to a war that the deaths of men on the battlefield are somehow futile or mistaken. This I take to be a truly religious wrath. It is connected with the supreme value, in the minds of even unreligious persons, of blood sacrifice. Once blood is shed, war takes on an aspect of the sacred and it is blasphemous to question the official 'truth'. Hence the shocking readiness of the general public in Britain and the United States to have the truth kept from them during the Gulf War.[4] People are not interested in truths which might interfere with their emotional identification of right and wrong, especially at the critical moment when the solidarity of violence is the highest value.[5]

War itself has a kinship with religion in what it demands of people and the way it heightens religious feelings. It does something to people which churches are always supposed to be trying to do: to promote selflessness and courage, to take people out of themselves and their own little designs and to make them live for something greater. It puts an end to the petty political squabbles which occupy them in peacetime. It gets people to lay down their lives for others. It has the capacity to make people feel really alive, because, for once they feel really part of something greater than themselves. Their solidarity with others is total and selfless while the violence lasts. It gives them an absolute, a totally demanding cause which relativises even life itself. People experience what has been accurately called 'the false transcendence of violence'.[6]

In this situation, religious leaders are in a dilemma. In the short run, they often see much to be gained by putting their authority behind the national war effort. But in the long run, the price for religion is enormous. By lending its weight to the conflict, religion takes on the goals and the methods of the state and its combatants. Acting in God's name it binds God to these goals and methods. The God they get, of course, is the God of Battles who fights for one group against another and who demands unlimited numbers of human lives: not the God of Abraham, Isaac and Jacob, not the God of Jesus Christ, nor Allah the merciful and just.

The willing sacrifice of the warriors soon becomes another kind of sacrifice which we have learned in the twentieth century to call 'holocaust'. This is a type of sacrifice which does not lend itself to heroism, to memorials, or to any attempt to make religious sense of it.[7]

I do not wish to imply that christians have learned nothing since the First World War. The row over the Falklands thanksgiving service and the failure of the Government to get any satisfactory victory celebration after the Gulf War indicates a radical shift of attitude in many christians which has affected even bishops and moderators. However, a country at war always needs the co-operation of religious leaders in the effort to unify the nation on an emotional and spiritual level. And many christians will still be tempted to identify loyalty to their country with loyalty to their God. Before hostilities broke out in the Gulf War, the Prime Minister invited both the Archbishop of Canterbury and Cardinal Hume along to No.10 for 'conversations'. They told the press it was a 'pastoral visit'. The claim that it was a *just war* was a claim about God's involvement. And how important it was to get an archbishop or a cardinal to say it!

A CHRISTIAN TRADITION OF DESACRALISING WAR

The rivalry for human souls between God and the state at war was clearly recognized by the Christians of the first three centuries. Their repudiation of military service has been explained in different ways, usually depending on the historian's position with regard to pacifism and just war. It has been described as morally-rigorous non-violence, faithful to the teaching of Jesus on the one hand, or as purely religious scruple about the idolatrous rituals associated with Roman military life on the other. Neither explanation does justice to the intimate connections between religion and warfare which the early christians perceived. 'No one can serve two masters': the second century christian writer Hermas applies this saying of Jesus to the conflict in the Christian's soul between God and the State. The pagan intellectual Celsus called this saying a 'seditious word of a people who wall themselves off and break away from the rest of mankind'.[8] At certain moments, it was impossible to serve both the State in its periodic absolute claims on the individual, and the Father of Jesus Christ, the maker of heaven and earth. In their choice of the latter, christians earned the description 'atheist', and 'enemies of the human race'. Indeed it was a kind of atheism — the kind that every Christian has to discover for herself at some point in life. It was a refusal to accept the claims of the little gods of this world, especially the gods invoked by the State in its violent rituals which were, after all nothing but a mystification and reification of the State itself. The order of this world was an idolatrous one, out of which they had been called. While they valued the peace secured by the Roman armies, they considered it temporary, not the peace of the kingdom of God, and not theirs to promote except by prayer.

So the central tradition of christian theology was established that believers are in exile in the State, or what Augustine called the earthly city. Augustine is regularly blamed for lots of things which have fallen out of favour, including the invention of the christian just war. But it does not appear to me, in reading the texts in which he speaks of war in *The City of God,* that he thought it was anything else than a tragic and deeply regrettable circumstance of this life of exile, which should make the christian yearn to reach the heavenly City, her true home. War belongs to the earthly, not the heavenly city, which is why the church may not defend itself by war.[9] He was considerably more sceptical about the just wars of the Christian Roman Emperors than other christians had been before him. Like the wars of ancient Rome, they too were mere glorified armed robberies. For others like Eusebius of Caesaria however, the conversion of Constantine had been the fulfilment of prophecy about the destruction of idols in the last times and the universal spread of the gospel. Roman wars against infidel barbarians could now be seen as God's wars. By the time he wrote the *City of God,* Augustine had ceased to accept that simple and fatally misleading version of sacred history.[10] He made it clear the warfare was not something which christians could wage for the sake of the church, let alone the City of God, which needed no such defence, but only because they had a kind of temporary duty to the city of their exile. There is an important sense in which Augustine began a tradition of *desacralisation* of war, which has always existed side by side with an altogether more dangerous and suspect tendency among Christians to sanction the idea of the holy war when waged by Christian government. I take it that one of the central elements of just war thinking since Augustine has been to desacralise war, to cut it down to size, to make it a fallible instrument of this-worldly justice with strict moral limits on its methods and scope, instead of a limitless crusade of the good against the evil, where those fighting on God's side are guaranteed the victory. It was for this reason that Classical just war writers in the Augustinian tradition, like Francisco Vitoria (fl. 1532), would not allow that difference of religion could be a cause of a just war.[11] This is a type of desacralisation one can only applaud. It should be carefully distinguished from *secularisation*. De-sacralisation I take to be part of what it means to believe in the God of Jesus Christ. For gentile believers it is an original effect of the gospel. It means getting rid of gods and leaving scope instead for belief in the God of the Jews, the creator of heaven and earth. Faced with the little gods of war, it seems to me that it is a duty of the Christian to de-sacralise as much as possible. Secularisation on the other hand is a slippery concept, difficult to define satisfactorily.[12] I take it to be a social process whereby the symbols of religious faith lose their meaning and God ceases to matter to everyday life. However, the wars of the twentieth century have revealed how religious passions persist underneath secularisation to re-emerge in times of crisis.

What we now see in our century is a progressive *re*-sacralisation of war. Far from discouraging it as it was meant to, the wide acceptance of just war doctrine appears to have encouraged it. A claim about justice is nowadays a claim about God's involvement.[13] Largely through the experience of the Gulf War, I have lost much of my former confidence that the Just War tradition can do our de-sacralisation of war for us. In all contemporary wars, religion has returned with a vengeance, and has largely co-opted the originally de-sacralising tradition of just war. The de-sacralising project of the Christian just war writers appears to have failed us, since the rise of nationalist passions and new absolutes has progressively re-sacralized war. It seems that the founding fathers of the just war tradition did not sufficiently appreciate the intimate, and perhaps unbreakable, connection between war and religion.

THE JUDGMENT OF WAR

If we want to repudiate the false religion of war, the question remains for us, just how does war stand in relation to God's providence and care for the world, which is part of our Christian faith. Of all things, war is the one where people are most likely to want to see the hand of God operating. And like love, war is such a powerful experience that it is likely to tell us something important about God. If we dismiss holy war ideas, one conceivable answer to this question is that war is a **judgment.**

This idea has Biblical precedents. The wars in which ancient Israel was defeated by the military super-powers of the time were interpreted by the prophets as judgments upon Israel's failure to lead a holy life in the land which God had given it — notably a failure to do justice to the poor. Israel's military defeats were said to be the consequence of her sins. The unjust society became indefensible, in more than one sense. God was not against war as such, but only declared that Israel could not win if it lived an unholy and idolatrous life. This included trying to worship God himself while oppressing the poor.

But this was only part of the answer. The defeat of Israel in war — especially the final defeat of the state of Judah and the exile in Babylon — gave scope for a new kind of faith: faith in the God who created heaven and earth, who was God of the Babylonians and Persians ('My anointed, Cyrus') as much as of Israel: the God who is in control of world history. So defeat in war, while being a judgment was also a revelation. The tribal god of Israel — the God of Battles — was transformed into something quite other. It was probably within this realisation that the biblical accounts of creation were put together. There were wars to come, and sometimes Israel relapsed into tribalism, but, through the prophetic reaction to defeat, the fundamental theology of the creator God was established — something quite new, something fatal to all the gods of this world, and something which would make all the difference to political theology. It was the experience of being a defeated people in Babylon which made both theology of the creator God and the theology of the two cities possible: both inherited by western Christianity, both receiving definitive shape in Augustine's *City of God.*

Nevertheless, the idea of war as judgment is not now applicable without severe modification. In the first place, no nation can call itself chosen by the creator God, as ancient Israel did, though the temptation has often been great. To do so would be to reclaim nothing but a tribal god. Consequently the idea of God's judgment cannot have the same force of a two-term relationship in crisis, or the consequence of the violation of a covenant, which is what it was for ancient Israel. Secondly, we cannot adopt the ancient way of viewing defeat as the judgment of God and victory as vindication. That again is a tribal way of looking at things and it is wholly out of place in modern war, where both victors and vanquished are usually devastated, and where large numbers of wholly innocent people on all sides are normally killed. Nevertheless, I think there are still senses in which war as such might be thought of as judgment. Along with most contemporary christians I would want to repudiate the idea of a God who sends war as a divine judgment for a sinful life in peacetime. But I do not think we need to see judgment in quite this personal way. There is plenty of scope for interpreting the Biblical language of God's wrath in an impersonal sense — in the sense of nemesis rather than punishment. [14]

What we can say about God then is something negative (which is normally the only kind of thing we can say about God, in any case). That is, that God does not intervene to rescue people from the consequences of their folly. This goes for collective folly as much as for individual folly. I have no difficulty in thinking of judgment as something inflicted upon nations as on individuals. The fact that this kind of judgment then involves suffering and death for a lot of innocent individuals in no way impugns the justice of God, since it is suffering and death inflicted by human beings on others (including those of their own side), which is simply the way things are in this world. War can be a judgment of a whole political culture — a culture, for instance which gives priority to armaments instead of feeding the hungry; which dedicates immense resources to short-term military strategies while nothing at all can be found for the long term strategies required for peace; where cultural superiority and the right of interference in the lives of backward peoples are assumed; where no one really gives a damn about the destruction of the natural environment. It is not difficult to see how the Gulf war was a judgment in this sense, although the achievement of 'victory' has obscured this for most people.

But besides judgment, there was usually — if not always — another side to the prophetic message: God's mercy. There is no support in the Bible, any more than there is in life, for the idea that God's mercy consists in rescuing people from the consequences of their folly. So what does it consist in? In biblical times, the mercy of God was often seen to be in the catastrophe itself. If it was not final, that is. It could be seen as a warning. Even as God's long-suffering and forbearance. An eye-opener. A chance — perhaps the very last chance — to change our way of life. According to Aquinas, the mercy of God is the grace God gives to some, beyond their common powers, to escape the mad dash for the abyss in which the rest of the world is caught up. It is the sin of presumption to think we can do this if we take no steps whatever to change direction. Even so, he says, it is a lesser sin than despair, since it is based on a lesser mistake about God: while punishment and judgment arise from human sin, mercy and forbearance arise from God's very nature; they are a result of her infinite goodness. [15]

1.   Remarks at the Annual Convention of the National Religious Broadcasters 28 January 1991.

2.   See the works of Rene Girard, especially *Violence and the Sacred, The Scapegoat,* and *Things Hidden from the Beginning of the World.*

3.   Explored with wit and learning by Alan Wilkinson in *The Church of England and the First World War,* SPCK 1978, and *Dissent or Conform? War Peace and the English Churches 1900-1945,* SCM Press, 1986.

4.   Shocking, for instance, to the BBC correspondent John Simpson, who has been responsible for much of the original reporting from Baghdad during the conflict.

5.   The truth-suppressing nature of violence is explored by Rene Girard in *Violence and the Sacred.*

6.   See Jean Bethke Elshtain in her powerful and unjustly-neglected work, *Women and War,* Harvester Press 1987.

7.   A theme I explored in 'Memory, Sacrifice and War', *New Blackfriars,* Nov. 1990, pp. 501-510.

8.   See Robert L. Wilken, *The Christians as the Romans Saw Them*, Yale University Press, 1984 pp 117-125. See also, Klaus Wengst, *Pax Romana and the Peace of Jesus Christ*, SCM Press 1987.

9.   *City of God* Bk 15.4 and 19.7

10.   For an excellent account of Augustine's de-sacralising political theology, see Robert Markus, *Saeculum: history and society in the theology of St. Augustine*, Cambridge University Press 1970.

11.   The object was to disqualify the wars waged against the heathens of the New World by the Conquistadores in the name of christianity. See Francisco Vitoria, *De Jure Belli*, 10, in *Classics of International Law*, Ed. Ernest Nys, Washington 1917 p 170.

12.   See Owen Chadwick, *The Secularization of the European Mind in the 19th Century*, Cambridge University Press, 1975.

13.   The religious claims made in modern war, including just war, have been very well discussed by James Mackey (see *Modern Theology*, OUP 1987, pp 170-189). He has pointed out that people who are ready to die and to kill in war are dealing in absolutes and are positing some kind of life beyond death. This may not be in the traditional form of personal survival — it could be for the lives of one's children or country. But in any case it amounts to a quasi-religious faith and hope similar in depth and power to that of traditional religion.

14.   See A.T. Hanson, *The Wrath of the Lamb*, SPCK 1957.

15.   *Summa Theologiae*, IIa IIae 21. 1c and 2c.

Section Three

Section Three represents Paul's commitment to the dispossessed of the earth — both on his doorstep and throughout the world at large. Andrew Hake's essay asks the sharp question — why are so few church members actively committed to issues of social justice? It was a question which Paul often asked and one which made him progressively more disillusioned with the institutional church. Andrew Hake's experience as a member of the Archbishop's Commission which produced the Faith in the City report gives him some special insights into some of the reasons which prevent churchgoing Christians from being in the vanguard of political and social change. He examines in particular the practical absence of a theology of the corporate and the consequences of this for action. Whilst charitable acts are central to the Christian's commitment, a commitment to campaign for justice for the poor is not. Horace Dammer's essay emerges from a long commitment to issues of social justice world wide and it focuses on global ecological concerns. Through the use of case studies, he relates the action required to attend to these concerns to a radical change of lifestyle, which must inform the committed Christian, if the whole human family is to be saved from the urgent dangers of the present state of global injustice. Horace Dammers links the issues of arms and armament to the urgent needs of the planet and calls for a bloodless revolution led by all those who can commit themselves to a true and fruitful poverty of spirit.

THE CHURCH'S INDIFFERENCE TO ISSUES OF SOCIAL INJUSTICE

Andrew Hake

INTRODUCTION

This essay will aim to explore a puzzle which has long troubled me. The issue lies behind many of the difficult questions on the urban agenda today to which Paul Baker's life and witness have spoken. The question is this: *Why is it that apparently so few church members are actively committed to issues of social justice?* I have in mind issues affecting the ordering of society, questions involving evident or latent conflict between organisations capable of using corporate power. By 'active commitment' I mean membership and sustained, regular public support for a campaigning body, for example, not only a political party, trade union or employers' organisation, but also groups who aim to change public policies and influence public opinion.

The evidence for such a thesis is not entirely informal, although my experience of discussions in congregations certainly bear it out. A survey carried out by the Bible Society 'into the beliefs, attitudes and opinions of the people of Swindon', published in 1987, offers more statistical support.[1] In response to the question 'Which of the following do you belong to?', only 7% of regular churchgoers (once a month or more) included 'Political Parties or groups', but this was significantly higher than the 1% of the 'occasional attenders' (Christmas, Easter only) and 4% of the 'never' attenders. Comparable figures for membership of 'Charities concerned with welfare' were 29%, 21% and 5%.

These figures, of course, bear out the widespread and sometimes sacrificial commitment of the most regular churchgoers to 'charity', to bodies alleviating the pains of injustice. But this only underlines the problem that *campaigning* organisations are (with widespread ambiguities) excluded from registration as charities. (This confusion is based on the theological error which fails to accept that justice is the way in which love works in the public domain of power conflicts. Our muddled legislative and administrative system helps to channel energies away from justice or social change and thus provides significant support for the *status quo*).

JUSTICE ISSUES

There is no attempt here to rank the merits of campaigning issues, although those listed here have massive scriptural justification, viz, the need for active commitment with people in poverty and other victims of injustice. The prior question is the evident refusal of more than nine out of ten active churchgoers to become practically involved in *any* social justice issue whatever. Behind this question there is the massive public complacency about the current ordering of British society.

In a turbulent world, most of us feel that, on the whole, Britain has got it about right. There are, of course, few people who would argue that there are **no** problems in British society which call for Christian concern — that all is well in the best of all possible worlds; and it would always be accepted that there are some issues of special interest to a minority of people, but these are not really worth serious campaigning by most of us.

Over against this general indifference, there is a current of awareness of justice issues in some parts of the churches. There are, for example, the public expressions of Church leaders, often of timely significance, but too often contradictory. The mind of the Church of England has been expressed through its synods: for example to the effect that much of the *'grave and fundamental injustice'* in urban priority areas described in *FAITH IN THE CITY* in 1985, still remains after some six years, while some more recent changes 'give cause for despair'.[2]

By 1991 the number of people in poverty had increased during the 1980s. The MORI survey publicised in *Breadline Britain 1990s* showed that the number of people in severe poverty — lacking seven or more necessities — increased from 2½ to 3½ million between 1983 and 1990.[3] Professor Townsend showed that 'Between 1979 and 1989, the income of the poorest fifth of the population is shown to have fallen by 4.6 per cent, while that of the richest fifth grew by almost 40 per cent.[4]

According to official government figures, 7,700,000 people were defined as being on 'less than half average income, the nearest thing to an official poverty benchmark'.[5]

"More people are living in relative poverty in the United Kingdom than in any other European Community country, according to a European Commission report". "On this report's definitions, some 10.3 million people, or 3.8 million households were living in poverty in Britain in the middle 1980s."[6]

Are we unable to 'hear' what statistics say to us?

Among those who experience exclusion from mainstream community life are most of the 2,500,000 people who were in June 1991 registered unemployed and many others who want but lack regular work.

Since 1985, 'the number of homeless people has increased, more dwellings have become unfit for habitation'[7], and although there has been an attempt to 'tidy up' the scandalous number of single homeless people sheltering in London's cardboard city, nothing fundamental has been done to tackle the basic causes of homelessness, especially in other urban centres.

Class-based ill-health raises sharp issues of injustice. People in poverty are sick more often and die younger. Those of all ages, (including infants), whose household head is an unskilled worker, people who are unemployed, or in social and material deprivation, suffer up to twice the rates of sickness and death, compared with the top groups in Britain. The gap has continued to widen since 1980.[8]

Although in 1990/91 some steps were at last taken to begin to tackle the conditions of Britain's prisons and the flaws in the legal system which were widely condemned by senior figures in the Establishment, it was agreed that it was going to take years before long-overdue changes could be introduced. Perhaps the most tragic victims of penal inhumanity and injustice were the growing number of teenagers who took their own lives in prison cells.

Widespread discrimination and humiliation is still inflicted unjustly on Britain's 'gay' minorities. While it will surely take time before faithful adult homosexual love is generally accepted in the Church, current social injustices are surely unacceptable to the Christian conscience.

The black and Asian population of Britain have for years protested against the racial prejudice and discrimination which have imposed hurt and injustice on individuals and communities, documented in report after report.

Many people who suffer real deprivations in our affluent society are part of the growing underclass, described by Professor Ralf Dahrendorf as 'the permanently poor and the long-term unemployed who found it virtually impossible to enter the labour market... The new minority cannot form itself into a class. It does not march on Westminster. If it is lucky, it finds a few people — and Prince Charles — who are its advocates. This growth of semi-citizens or second class citizens who are marginalised and who cannot defend themselves is a most serious development.'[9]

My question is this: Why is it that so few of the most regular churchgoing Christians are members of groups such as Church Action on Poverty, the Child Poverty Action Group, Shelter, the Prison Reform Trust, the Howard League or similar campaigning bodies? How many congregations are affiliated to such organisations? How many clergy place issues such as poverty or racism on the agenda for congregational discussion and action?

Overshadowing this tragic national catalogue of deprivation is a global context which makes Britain's difficulties seem almost trivial. That there is a problem of (so-called) 'Third World' debt is generally known. What is scarcely acknowledged is our share of responsibility in Britain for the suffering that is being ruthlessly imposed on poorer nations. Christian Aid states that 'UNICEF estimates that half a million children are dying each year because of economic pressures created by debt'.[10] 'On present trends, over 100 million children will die in the 1990s — 50 million of them from just three common diseases which can be inexpensively treated or prevented'.[11]

Debt and interest repayments in 1988, the latest year for which figures are available, totalled $178 billion — three times as much as all the aid received from the industrialized countries.[12] This was more than aid, grants and new loans together. *There is therefore a massive net flow of resources from the poor South to the rich North of the planet.*

We in Britain properly express horror at the slave trade inflicted on millions of African people before, during and after the eighteenth century, and at the Holocaust on six million Jews and others by the Third Reich. Is it not time we opened our eyes and hearts to the institutional Holocaust being carried out in our name through the consequences of 'adjustment policies' being imposed by the agents of the rich nations — principally the International Monetary Fund — against tens of millions of the most vulnerable people in the poorest countries of the world in order to sustain our own standard of living? Are we not in the same position as the pious German Christians who turned a blind eye to the Final Solution? Yet our donations to international charities, which indeed relieve some of the symptoms, provide only £1 for ever £9 provided through government sources. Why is it, then, that such a tiny handful of people and congregations actively support the World Development Movement which campaigns to increase government aid and to change official policies in order to tackle the causes of international injustice?

WHY NOT? — What people say

1.   'We care, but we're not sufficiently convinced'. The victims are hidden, we have not met them face-to-face; are they really complaining? Are the needs as serious as the publicists suggest? Is it really hurting? Is this perhaps a campaign on the part of people with an axe to grind?

We should ask ourselves why the victims of injustice appear not to be in our congregations in Comfortable Britain, not part of our social circle. It is not easy to organise face-to-face presentations of examples of injustice. The leap from caring to being active in social campaigning is not easy to take; it is much harder than taking the step from not caring to being a charitable giver.

2. 'We care, of course, but social issues are not our priority; we are not many in our congregation, and we have to give our energies to keeping the church going.' Different people with varying temperaments are best engaged in appropriate tasks. 'Campaigning is not my scene' But this may, or course, cover other motives; one may feel that giving priority to institutional maintenance is exactly the policy challenged by *FAITH IN THE CITY*.

3. 'Of course we care, but it is all too complicated'. So many issues of injustice are indeed extremely complex, and it is surely part of our discipleship not to rush to ill-informed or hasty judgements. Serious action for justice depends on the hard work and intellectual commitment of people who are prepared to read about the issues. Does such a remark imply elitism? It is fair for committed people to ask that the essential elements of important issues should be accessible without immersion in a mass of detail. Much may depend upon which newspaper we read, and, indeed, how far we are aware of the slant it gives to the presentation of news. Is this something for our Church teaching programmes? The presentation of issue-sheets by, for example, a Board for Social Responsibility can be helpful, although 'objective' summaries are seldom as cogent as those prepared by campaigning organisations. What difference would they make? Would they be welcomed by the congregation or left in a heap on the table at the back of the church? What is in the bookstall? Who actually buys, borrows, reads?

4. 'We care, but some of these issues are all too remote.' But is it not astonishing that the Church of all organisations should be so slow to accept the global perspective? Our generation is the first to have to face daily the planetary dimension of social issues. Poverty in Britain is structurally tied in with world poverty — the same factors are at work around the globe. The same goes for ecological and 'green' questions, and nuclear issues. Chernobyl recognised no frontiers. Nor, in the last resort, does AIDS. Unemployment is affected by international markets, and the activities of transnational firms reach into the village communities of Britain.

A crucial factor in the level of personal commitment to campaigning bodies is therefore the existence of local groups. The churches have the most complete network of local groups in the British Isles. In realistic terms, however, it is organisations such as Amnesty International and Friends of the Earth who can say to an enquirer 'Come along on Thursday evening' — so that practical engagement convinces the potential activist that they are part of something worthwhile and relatively effective. National organisations which find it hard to develop local groups are those who find it hard to point to concrete projects for local involvement. This suggests a priority for building small committed groups at very local level.

5. 'Yes, I want to do something, but not with those people'. 'Politics is a dirty game, and Christians should not get mixed up with people who have conflicting motives'. The proper place for compromise and alliances for justice is an aspect of Christian teaching which needs much more attention than it has received, and we return to it below.

6. 'There are so many issues, that we can't get involved in them all'. Whilst this is the proper plea of the activist who has to face the issue of priorities between justice issues and tries to avoid the dissipation of energies, it can be an excuse for 'privatisation' or mere inaction by others.

7. 'We try to be involved but we feel powerless'. 'What real difference do we make?' 'Nobody much listens.' This is the reaction which is taken seriously by the Community Organising movement, which achieves some success in generating commitment in congregations which have previously not ventured into social justice issues. Using a formula that has met with some success in the United States, Community Organising begins by intensive one-on-one interviews to raise awareness of the potential of a coalition of campaigning groups and discerning the issues on which members of congregations feel most concern. Community Organising works on the principle of concentrating on 'winnable issues'. Successes do, indeed, mean encouragement. But it is a matter of judgment whether Christians should not take up 'unwinnable' issues of injustice even in the face of what appears to be insuperable hostility. After all, there are sometimes surprise developments in human affairs (South Africa and Eastern Europe come to mind). Nevertheless, if Community Organising is helping Christians and congregations to become involved in authentic justice issues, it will be helping to raise awareness and challenge some prejudices.

It is also clear that a gift to charity promises that one's money will probably be used quickly and effectively. By comparison, energy given to campaigning does not promise a quick or even an effective outcome. Waiting for the verdict of history, and even the satisfaction that 'we were right' does not offer practical remedy to victims or prevent further injustice meanwhile. There are certainly an unknown number of 'hidden' lobbying letter-writers and subscribers to justice movements whose commitment is not made public.

If your MP is not sympathetic or is committed to a policy one believes to be unjust, there is little evident effect to be gained by writing to him or her. One is locked into a hostile political environment. (This suggests the value of two-member constituencies, where at least there can be a possible alternative. No wonder existing MPs oppose the idea.)

Those who belong to a political party find that the effect one can have on the system is usually extremely remote, unless one works one's way into the inner circles of the organisation, an extremely time-consuming business. And the closer one gets to the centres of power, even in the House of Commons, the greater the feeling, one understands, that the 'really important' decisions are made by a small caucus.

Our democratic system means that most people have very little awareness of, and feel very little responsibility for, many of the things that are done in their name. How many Christians confess the corporate sin of Britain in the injustices of the penal system or of 'Third World' debt, for example? These questions point to national political malaise, with cynicism about the value of the vote, and the entire process of delegated decision-making. Can it be right for Christians to drop out of the democratic process? To these questions we return below.

Such reflections take us some of the way in getting to the heart of our exploration. But there is a deeper sickness within the Church which must be considered.

TEACHING:

The lapse of the Church into Marcionism

In our generation, we have distorted the faith in a Marcionite fashion. Marcion was the son of the Christian bishop of Sinope in Pontus on the Black Sea, who came to Rome around 140 A.D. He was so deeply convinced of the newness and grandeur of Christianity that he could not believe that both the Jewish Law and the love of Jesus Christ could arise from the same God. Jesus, he taught, came from the God of Love to abolish the law and the prophets, and conquered the 'inferior God of the Jews'. The Marcionites produced their own Bible, eliminating the Old Testament, all epistles except ten of St. Paul, and including only an edited gospel of Luke. They had some Gnostic elements in their strict discipline, and were a popular and effective heretical movement with their own martyrs, having churches, bishops and presbyters up to the seventh century. The similarities with some present-day Christianity are striking.[13]

Some Christians may feel that 'all these injustices are sent to try us', and there is little we can or should do to strive against the will of God. 'There will be wars and rumours of war', famines and so on. Our proper response, it is suggested, is to accept all things with thanksgiving. There must be, however, a distinction between mere fatalism on the one hand and, on the other, the realism of accepting the given facts of a situation as a starting point, the raw material of mission, and trying to change them with the motive of love.

Others will protest that the 'justice-campaigning mode is not the appropriate Christian response to injustice.' 'Jesus refused the temptation to organise campaigns for economic, political or popular power' (Lk.4.1-13; Matt.4.3-10).

Jesus was born into a society which had for centuries been deeply committed to the covenant and sovereignty of Yahweh over the whole life of the nation, individual and corporate. Telling evidence of the life of Jesus and his social attitudes between the ages of twelve (Lk.2.42) and about thirty (Lk.3.23) has to be inferred from the silence of the gospel narratives.

He was working as an artisan, evidently a prayerful synagogue-attender, with a perceptive knowledge of the scriptures. If he had challenged the law, or been other than a "normal", law-abiding citizen, it seems inconceivable that this would not have been mentioned in the gospels. Until his baptism by John (Matt.3.13-17 and parallels), Jesus evidently led the life of an "ordinary" Galilean. Unless we accept the theories of adoptionism (That Jesus was adopted as Son of God at his baptism), long rejected by the church, we must as Christians accept the very remarkable fact that the Son of God amazingly experienced a "wholly ordinary" and evidently unremarkable human, adult life for 15-20 silent years before 'he arrived at the Jordan from Galilee' and his ministry began. This is a double affirmation of incarnation as radical human embodiment.

After his baptism, Jesus embarked on the work recorded in the gospels. It is surely obvious that he did not need to spell out those aspects of the life and culture of his society which he still affirmed. With so much else to be told, these aspects could evidently be taken for granted. The provisions in the Jewish Law for social justice and the care of the needy, for worship and family life remained in place.

Jesus refused to become personally involved in adjudicating in disputes between individuals (Lk.12.13f), warning contestants in the first place against personal covetousness, and by implication referring them to the existing Jewish systems of adjudication.

It was only when his radical challenges to human attitudes seemed to suggest that he could be undermining the whole system of law and justice, that he had to explain that he had come, not to destroy the system of the law and the prophets, but to fulfil it, (see Matt.5.17) — meaning that law and the system of administering justice must be affirmed as necessary for the right ordering of any society, (together with prophets to "ad-just" it), in the light of the whole Old Testament experience.

Of course he had to add that the system of law fell far short of the Kingdom, needing to be filled full of people and groups with attitudes embodying God's love. It was also clear to Jesus that Israel's understanding of the Law (the *Torah*, 'instruction') had been allowed to degenerate into an arid legalism which too often put the letter of the law (and the power of those in control of the law) above the loving purposes of God in response to the needs of people. The Sabbath, he had to point out, was made for humankind and not *vice versa*.

Law, in short, was the way that love becomes effective in the public life of institutions 'until the last day'. As St. Paul clearly emphasised, the Law was not what the Jews had believed — the royal highway to acceptable status in the divine purpose.

Jesus's affirmation of the provisional place of the system of law in society is thus *assumed* in the four gospels. For this reason, the main (but far from exclusive) emphasis in the gospels is on encounters with individuals and both personal and corporate attitude-changing. This emphasis on loving motives was radical, but not really new.

Clearly Jesus was not a party politician, not a Zealot. He took the parties of Israel seriously and took sides (for example, Matt. chapter 23), but was never identified with any. He was crucified by Pilate as a political rebel.[14] In other words, Jesus did not march alongside the activists aiming to deal with injustice by changing policies or power systems in the conventional 'democratic' ways. He went to the roots of both individual and corporate injustice by confronting it with the love of God, with the Kingdom, in his own person. This, however, is too often wrongly taken by the church today as calling for a utopian stance, "above" the rough and tumble of conflicts. The error of this interpretation becomes apparent, when it is recognised that Jesus confronted the authorities in such a resolute and effective way that they decided he had to be eliminated.

How else are we to explain Jesus's frequent challenges to whole groups of people? What are we to make of his plea to 'Jerusalem, Jerusalem', to other cities, to the *collective* attitudes and practices of parties such as 'this generation' or 'the Pharisees,' and to the final climax of his ministry in his deliberate confrontation of the power leadership of the nation in the Temple — the central (and also the major economic and employing) institution in the land? (See, for example: Lk.13.34f., 19.41-44, 9.41, 10.10-15, 11.29-32, 11.39-52, Chapters 20-24, and parallels in other Gospels).

By dying for both the victims of injustice and its perpetrators, and in his resurrection, as Jurgen Moltmann puts it:

> "he revealed a new righteousness which breaks through the vicious circles of hate and vengeance and which from the lost victims and executioners creates a new mankind with a new humanity ... Only where creative love changes what is hateful and deserving of hate... can one speak of the true revolution of righteousness." In other words, he promised God's "law of grace for the unrighteous and self-righteous alike."[15]

Many of the parables of Jesus refer clearly to the Jewish nation, its promise and its betrayals, and in no way only to individuals. Clearly Jesus was well aware that human individual and community belong to each other and that there is an indissoluble and very subtle dialectic between them.

As Lesslie Newbigin has said: 'There is, there can be, no private salvation, no salvation which does not involve us with one another'.[16] How is it that the Church has failed to produce a clear and cogent image of Jesus as powerfully and painfully involved in challenging the corporate sin of injustice, and as providing a mandate and model for Christians to be so involved in ways which are consistent with his style?

Perhaps part of the answer lies in understanding the different ways in which the word justice has been interpreted. Julio de Santa Ana has pointed out that "In Western tradition, and in its Jewish and Greek sources, there are two ideas of justice. The first, in the Old Testament, affirms that God executes justice from below, that is, from the level of the oppressed. The second, in line with Greek beliefs, represents justice as a goddess with bound eyes, a sword in her right hand and a balance in her left — the two pans of the balance being at the same level. Thus in this view, justice is understood as neutral and equidistant from the parties to the dispute.[17] In its history since the first Pentecost, the Church has faced many situations which have involved facing up to the different interpretations of justice. When the Roman Emperor became a Christian, early in the fourth century AD, the attempt was made, however often deeply flawed when viewed with hindsight, to bring the ordering of society under the rule of the Kingdom of God. But through the ages Christians have, from time to time, been so convinced that those in power, even Christians, were ruling unjustly, that they have as Christians at the risk of their lives joined together in peaceful or violent opposition.

Now that we live in a democratic society, claiming, however inadequately, that those in power are answerable to the people, an even greater obligation rests on Christians who have the opportunity to try to bring the insights of the love of Christ to bear on the ordering of society. In our society, is not campaigning an essential element in loving our neighbour?

THE ETHOS OF THE CHURCH

At the outset, we may have to accept that the conventional pattern of congregational life militates against any serious commitment to justice issues. In the Church of England, for example, what opportunities are offered for adequate engagement with justice questions at the parish communion or at a family service, timed carefully not to run much over the hour? A special meeting for interested people on a different day will attract only the few enthusiasts. Some house groups

64

are able to manage this successfully, but when can the congregation wrestle with serious issues of justice, hear well-prepared information, share views, receive reports and make decisions? Serious engagement cannot be squeezed into a bare 20 minutes in place of the sermon. With little space allowed for those who hunger and thirst after justice, their efforts tend to be marginalised and devalued in the life of the church. The exceptions tend to be when the direct interests of the Church are threatened — any squeeze on religious broadcasting for example is properly resisted, and Keep Sunday Special petitions will also sometimes be encouraged. A significant number of congregations give systematic backing to 'LIFE' campaigns, in opposition to abortion — an important expression of Christian conscience, though such congregations, if I am not mistaken, tend not be commited to some of the other justice issues, such as those spelt out above.

It is interesting to explore the gender dimension of this thesis. At the risk of sweeping generalisations it has to be accepted that on the whole, with extremely significant exceptions, it has been men who have given primary energy and concern to collective issues of, for example, trade union and political activity. But behind these perceptions lie cultural factors and negative consequences so powerful in a patriarchal society, issues revealed in much women's writing. Today the scene is changing, with women becoming increasingly 'politicised'. It might be important therefore to explore how far this change is reflected within congregations. Women comprise the great majority of churchgoers. Perhaps a traditional concern for personal and family dimensions of life has militated in the past against commitment to wider justice issues, and would account for the wider involvement in *LIFE* campaigning. Although the Mothers' Union has a notable tradition of commitment to justice issues, one must ask how far this emerges as practical commitment by rank-and-file members. In wider 'green' organisations women are extremely active. Perhaps as the social and political agenda of women changes, this changed agenda will gradually permeate the agenda of the Church and may change priorities and approaches, as well as the scale of operation. But this has to be seen as a very long-term hope.

The ordination of women in the Church of England and the Roman Catholic Church may not therefore be so far removed from the concerns of this article, for the clergy have a central role, both in the problem as defined and in any suggestions for tackling it. There is no question of the significance in practice and in witness of the sustained pastoral commitment of many priests and ministers, (including of course deacons and lay people of both genders). As with personal and collective charity, such pastoral work offers an important sign of Christian concern, and a paradigm of the quality of personal caring which 'justice' organisations cannot normally offer. Having acknowledged that fact however, it has to be made clear that clergy have a crucial influence on the ethos of congregations, and they have it in their power to support or pass by any attempts to encourage a campaigning approach to the issues of justice.

But the dilemma of parish clergy and of ministers responsible for congregations is acute. They are under very strong pressures to meet contradictory expectations, especially as those individuals most committed to the congregation are often the people most opposed to radical change or social involvement. The strong forces driving us to conform to the present systems of the Church act to deter the minister from expending the immense psychological energy demanded of any leader who tries to reach outside the dominant paradigm. This makes it very hard to minister seriously and systematically to the growing numbers of 'Christians outside the Church' beyond a conscientious ministry around the occasional offices. It means that we fear controversy and shy away from conflict. Understandably a minister is wholly reluctant to face division and desertion, and even the possibility of the ultimate financial 'ruin' of the congregation. Only a few very determined and courageous priests refuse to make it their business to 'seek peace' (where there is no true peace), and to make sure that contentious issues of 'justice' are not pushed to the margins. How many parishes really give any priority to Justice and Peace issues? As John A.T. Robinson once said, clergy tend to act as thermostats, effectively cutting off the power if the heat gets too great.

Even so wise a leader as Michael Ramsey somehow colluded in the contemporary climate of marginalising issues of justice. In his book *The Gospel in the Catholic Church,* he states: 'God proposes to unite mankind through a particular people, and to unite them, not in a programme of philanthropic and social progress, but in the worship of Himself.'[18] Such muddled language poses a false antithesis between a faithful worshipping Church or an alternative smeared as an untheological, political organisation tarred with the brush of an outdated secular optimism. Surely our aim should be a Christ-like Church standing as a sign to the world of the presence of the Holy Spirit at work in human lives?

When the final report of the Archbishop's Commission on Urban Priority Areas was being signed unanimously and submitted, I felt it right to send a personal but not confidential note to the Archbishop and to other members of the Commission. In the note was stated my conviction that "the situation in the Urban Priority Areas calls for a quite fundamental reordering of our society on a scale and at a depth which have implications far beyond the terms of reference of the Commission." Among other points, I urged that "in faithfulness to those who are suffering we should acknowledge more clearly the need for profound change in our national and global economic systems and in the values they embody at present." Furthermore, I suggested that "the Church remains too comfortably and uncritically enmeshed and aligned with the dominant groups in Britain. If the Church is to be truly a sign of the Kingdom and love of God in our society, the longer-term implications of the changes required are more radical and more painful than have been spelt out. The hand of history lies heavily upon the Church of England and the pressures towards conformity are strong. Consequently it is most important that we should not minimise the gap between the present pattern of the Church's life and that of a Church shaped afresh to engage in the divine mission in our own day.''

Bishop John Baker of Salisbury challenged the Anglican clergy of Bristol in 1989 in these words: "We have connived and colluded in the perversion of the Church, in turning it away to false objectives. We have not led our fellow Christians out into the world, we have tried to lure the world into the church. We have not helped our fellow Christians rescue the world, a world of industry and commerce, of government, of international relations, from darkness. We have settled for the self-regarding objective of bringing more people into Sunday services and church activities... And God has answered us. The people have not come in. Even in the so-called Age of Faith, only 25% of the population of this country went to church. Is it not time we dropped most of what we are doing and started to ask what Jesus wants done, and what changes His Spirit would tell us to make if we were not too frightened to listen? What God wants is for his world to be made into the land of the Trinity by the methods of the Incarnation.''

We have to break the idea that concern for justice issues is an 'additional extra' in the life of the church, permissible for people who are keen on that sort of thing. It has to be expected of all of us if we are being faithful to the commandment to love our neighbour, even if we dare to call ourselves Christians at all. Our commitment to worship is called under judgment in the Bible, if we fail to try to work it out beyond the church doors.

We are all caught up in this failure. Perhaps we have peeped behind the curtain, over the edge of the abyss, and are terrified by the radical implications of addressing the injustices we see. Are we serious in our intent, our rhetoric? Or do we convict ourselves of self-justification — ('Well at least I've tried to do my bit') or image-building, in other words, of hypocrisy?

THE ETHOS OF BRITISH SOCIETY

We are caught up in the Church as it is, and we are caught up in the dominant culture of our society. We mostly accept the normal assumptions of liberal democracy — with varying reservations. For example, 'that society is made up of separate, sovereign, atomistic individuals'.[19] The notion that 'there is no such thing as society', though widely challenged, found resonance with many British people. When Swindon Town Football Club was relegated as a means of disciplinary action in 1990, following the admission of long-term and systematic financial cheating by some of the Board of Directors, management and players, the pages of the local newspaper were full of protests along the lines 'Why should innocent fans be punished for the sins of a few individuals?' The fans, including myself, had rejoiced publicly together at the collective achievement of the team and the club in reaching, what was then the First Division. But any idea of later accepting corporate responsibility for the calculated wrongdoing which lay behind tht success was simply disclaimed in a chorus blaming 'individuals', — the people we left to get on with it on our behalf.

Our society thus finds it hard to accept the corporate dimension of life, the fact that we are all bound up with each other, mostly need each other, and have responsibility for each other. Any concept of corporate sin and justice is swept away in a tide of rampant individualism. Something of this spirit lies behind the Christian reluctance to engage in justice issues.

A second assumption of liberal democracy is that, in a plural society, justice is most likely to emerge from the free interplay of competing interests. Such an assumption underlies the argument for Christian participation in campaigning activities. But caution is called for. In the first place "all human causes are ambiguous and all human actions are involved in the illusions which are the product of our own egotism."[20]

If we see our way beyond the first ambiguities that strike us, we find ourselves standing alongside the professional lobbyists who are now part of our democratic system, and it is clear that their influence depends to a large extent on the financial pull of the interests they represent. To call for full declaration of interests and influences does not allay the fears of the weaker groups who may well stand for the greater needs of a wider public interest. Is it then the task of the Church to promote stronger lobbies for 'justice'? Was the Bishop of Durham far from the mark when he called for the Church Urban Fund to be set up as a 'fighting fund' to influence public opinion to remedy the injustices identified in *FAITH IN THE CITY?*

The alternatives to pressure group pluralism can, however, be even more sinister — some form of monolithic paternalism or totalitarianism. The flaws in the conventional "51:49" democratic system too often deny justice to minorities. As Jurgen Moltmann has said: "The crucified God is in fact a stateless and classless God. But that does not mean that he is an unpolitical God. He is the God of the poor, the oppressed and the humiliated. The rule of the Christ who was crucified for political reasons can only be extended through liberation from forms of rule which make men servile and apathetic and the political religions which give them stability."[21]

To quote Lesslie Newbigin again: True humanity, he argues, cannot be understood apart from a context in the public history of a particular time. "It is totally wrong, therefore, to separate the private from the public areas of human life and thereby remove politics from the sphere of Christian responsibility. To work for the reformation of structures, to expose and attack unjust structures, and, when the point is reached at which all other means have failed, to work for the overthrow of an evil political and economic order, is as much a part of the mission of the church as to care for the sick and feed the hungry. Part of it but not the whole.''[22]

If our problem is a reluctance to become involved in the process of campaigning for justice, somewhere near the heart of the matter is the extent to which we have been conformed to consumer society. We find ourselves entrapped, locked into the systems of credit, of expectations, of wasteful and polluting consumption which depends on the exploitation of the twothirds world and the exclusion of the substantial underclass in Britain. It is extraordinarily difficult to escape from being thus enmeshed, either as individuals, as families or collectively. But how hard are we trying? Our failure to analyse the issues, our collusion in our comfortable privileges amount to a basic betrayal in which we have made our own comfort and security the overriding priority. Whatever is the 'bottom line', the absolute essential, is the 'god' which a society worships. In Britain we Christians are involved in a massive idolatry. What is to be done?

SOME POSSIBLE WAYS FORWARD

Sharp challenges are raised here for the institutional Churches, especially for the established Church of England, which has the immense reponsibility of confronting the State in word and deed with the demands and opportunities of the Kingdom of God facing us today. If, as a nation, we are involved in national and planetary injustice on a stupendous scale, voices calling for justice should at least be heard, and endorsed so far as possible by the whole ecumenical body. Within the Church of England, the instruments of synodical government seem at present a long way from fulfilling this role.

Could it be that the most scriptural expression of the Decade of Evangelism would be a radical expression of corporate repentance? How this would be expressed in the style of Jesus raises a host of problems. Such a challenge to conventional opinion would probably be extremely unpopular in terms of filling pews. But it could be the most authentic proclamation of what the Christian faith actually involves.

The central question remains: *Is a commitment to work for justice seen as part of the essential work of the Church?* The central insight also remains: *that worship without any expression in corporate love — as well as individual love — is not authentic Christian worship, and that love means a commitment to collective justice in society.* To embrace these truths calls for immense courage on the part of the leaders of any congregation.

In other words, *What does it mean to reshape the Church around Kingdom issues, the Kingdom agenda?*

'From the time of Constantine and the Christianization of Europe Christianity has taken over the role of the political religion of society. It has in turn been politicized in accordance with the standards of the reasons of state which have obtained at various times... To make present one who was once crucified in the name of bourgeois religion means to replace bourgeois religion in a society with the churches as institutions which freely criticize society.'[23]

Since the task is so difficult, we should not therefore expect too much from the institutional churches, however much we must hope for and work for change. Perhaps the present role of such bodies in leading public opinion in directions towards embodying the Kingdom of God, is to be a little way ahead of the public and political centre of gravity in struggling for humanisation; to be within reach of what is realistically negotiable with those who formulate the conventions and rules of society. *FAITH IN THE CITY* in its recommendations to the nation, worked along these lines. Such influence — including the presence of bishops (or ecumenical church and multi-faith leaders) in the House of Lords — is not to be despised.

But a much more radical presence is also needed. Peter Marris in his most creative book *Meaning and Action,* has described the immense power of the giant transnational corporations and the impossible assumptions of sustained (and often destructive) economic growth on which their dominance depends. How, he asks, can such power be challenged? In order to be able to predict and manage the relationships of everyday life, we all tend to accept and reinforce the constraints which restrict our behaviour — even sometimes if such constraints are unjust. By making such deliberate acts of conformity we reinforce the structures of power; this process 'depends, then, on whether people go on believing that they must conform to them.' Movements of social change, which, in the first instance, commanded scarcely any material resources have become powerful through the force of their moral appeal', and 'characteristically begin to mobilize support through the action of a few people foolhardy enough to resist intimidation and withstand the consequences. They show that it is possible to act differently. What they represent now has to be chosen or rejected.'[24]

This analysis, I believe, has much to say to those committed to working for justice in society through the church. As John Baker has suggested, this will in the nature of things be a minority, or rather a network of minority voices and groups, working on the frontiers, on Kingdom issues of social justice, exploring radical solutions, facing costly opposition because they will be challenging the comfortable security and assumptions of both the church and the consumer society to which it is so remarkably conformed. Such groups and their members are likely to have differing relationships with the institutional churches, as have the various religious communities in the past. They will probably attract some of the 'Christians outside the Churches', as well as some within. They may draw the lines of 'doctrine' at different points and probably will have alliances with others who may profess no

Christian allegiance, but in the course of a common pursuit of justice, there will be opportunities for witness in both word and lifestyle. Theirs will be a radical ecumenism, and many will want to break bread together, even outside the conventions of some denominations. After all, as a good Roman Catholic friend said to me 'Who makes the rules? Whose supper is it?' It may therefore not be out of place to call them 'para-churches', and they will, I believe, be the growing edge of the Church.

Such groups bring into question the widespread conviction — which I must admit I have long shared — that we should always be able to generalise our convictions; in other words, to answer the quesiton: 'If everyone did this what would be the consequences for society?' For example, the Society of Friends has had immense influence towards the peaceful resolution of conflicts, as a creative Christian minority from the seventeenth century onwards. The pacifist witness of the Quakers, however, cannot be dismissed as irrelevant or as utopian simply because it has to be admitted that (as the Old Testament and parts of the New indicate) no society can be maintained on any scale, without an element of force, albeit most tightly controlled. Let the para-churches, therefore, not be afraid of a few 'extreme' absolutes, some 'utopian' and 'unrealistic' 'impossibilities', in order to keep our eyes, for some of the time at least on the vision of the Kingdom which has inspired the followers of Christ down through the centuries. What seems certain, however, is that the para-churches will have to struggle for all the necessities of support. As a wise friend once remarked, 'Prophecy has never been a very well-paid calling'. And the gift for which we must pray above all is courage.

OTHER SHOTS IN GOD'S LOCKER?

But when we have done all, and have not flagged nor retreated into pietism, we must nevertheless be realistic. This means that we do not entertain any facile optimism about the likely outcomes of our campaigning efforts, and do not succumb to depression in the face of what seems to be implacable opposition. But that does not leave us without hope.

Two very important strands of thought in the New Testament are necessary to our own thinking. The first is that history does not move along simple, smooth lines of cause and effect. Neither the Bible nor contemporary history supports any notion of steady progress towards the Kingdom of God. Changes and developments of course there are, but they are deeply ambiguous, embodying some qualitative steps towards the Kingdom and some demonic elements. The stream of human events which we call history moves by sudden discontinuities as well as quiet development or decline. The Bible speaks of these discontinuities as 'apocalyptic' — meaning basically a sudden uncovering of reality, of truth, which had until then been hidden.

To suggest that our future is likely to be apocalypctic need not mean a terminal nuclear event for the planet. What is much more inevitable for us in Britain, as part of Western culture and the rich Northern industrial society is that we are deeply under judgement for our ruthless and cruel economic manipulation of the poorer countries and of the poorest people in those countries. We cannot, we will not, hear the word which the Lord speaks to us. But God will affirm his justice in his own time. His Church must meanwhile offer a very sharp analysis, a very clear statement of the truth and the reality, and be prepared to be caught in the very painful and unpredictable suffering of the apocalyptic event. This is likely to entail a more costly witness than most of us are prepared to make at present.

The word 'capitalism' is a taboo word in the church. Merely to use it triggers off an instant expectation that it will be followed by a flow of socialist sloganising. This taboo has to be broken — by thoughtful and realistic people who recognise that our present economic system will have to be drastically changed within the next few years. There are good reasons for saying this. We have less than a decade before the creeping ecological crisis gets on top of us. During that time it will become clear that 'free' investment by transnational organisations on existing free market assumptions will be causing planetary ecological disasters, which it may by then be too late to repair, in terms of global warming, desertification, forest destruction and climate changes.

It is far from clear that democratic systems will be able to cope with the conflicts between the insistent, guzzling car-owning demands of a consumer society, and the imperatives to limit prodigal energy consumption for the common good. There will be increasingly sharp divergences between regimes reluctantly attempting to introduce very painful change by consensus and those resorting to authoritarianism to suppress dissent from the have-nots. We in the industrial countries are already engaged in such a conflict, on a world-wide scale. The suppression of our own underclass is one aspect of the same pattern, imposed with skilful media presentation, and an element of ruthlessness.

There may still be a chance that the ordering of British and Western European societies might follow a social democratic pattern with acceptance of very much more radical sharing than politicans have yet dared to propose.[25]

In our lifetimes — perhaps around 1960 — the consumer society has peaked and gone over the top, leaving millions of people behind facing increasing poverty, penury, destitution and famine. The question is whether the churches can accept that the lifestyle and message of Jesus is calling us to adopt in practice what the Christian Church has preached for so long and practised so fitfully. To admit that we cannot accept this, is to deny the reality of resurrection and to abandon our faith.

72

The word of Jesus to his friends linked with the apocalyptic passages in St Mark's Gospel, was 'Watch and pray'. This may sound like a classic retreat into pietism. But if it is spelt out as 'Be vigilant in reading the signs of the times, and be sensitive to what the Holy Spirit is saying to you', it can affirm us in our work for justice, and release us from any illusion that the outcome is essentially in our own hands.

There is a second strand of thinking in the New Testament which refers to the principalities, powers, dominions, potentates, lordship, thrones, angels, authorities, rudiments, elements, elementary spirits, and ruling spirits of the universe — which Leslie Newbigin discusses at some length in *The Gospel in a Pluralist Society,* from which I here draw heavily.[26] Some of these phrases come from contemporary Greek science, meaning the basic material structures which make up the universe. But Paul sees them also as invisible, though immensely powerful, 'spiritual' structures which have such an influence on human societies.

Newbigin draws out Paul's emphasis that these are part of God's creation for our good (Col.1.16). 'Our life in society is structured by law, custom and tradition. Without these we could not develop into responsible beings... There has to be some kind of ordered structure of power. Without it, human life would dissolve into anarchy. These structural elements are necessary to guide and protect human life. They serve God's purpose. But as we well know, they can also become demonic.' In fact Paul sees them as responsible for the death of Jesus. On the cross he triumphed over them (Col.2.15,20), they were defeated but not destroyed, and now 'every power and authority in the universe is subject to him as head' (Col,2.10; Eph.1.20-22).

This theology speaks powerfully to our contemporary situation. We find ourselves subject to such 'powers' as the world economic system, the media, the market. No single individual or indeed institution can be held responsible for the interlocking structures of power. Yet these 'powers' work through individuals and institutions, but are somehow, over, above, behind, them. They are realities; they are very powerful; they are ambiguous, both necessary yet potentially inhuman. 'Our struggle is not against human foes, but against cosmic powers, against the authorities and potentates of this dark age, against the superhuman forces of evil in the heavenly realms.' (Eph.6.12).

A vital part of any Christian campaigning against injustice must include these insights as central in its theology. The battle has already been won and 'sovereignty over the world has passed to our Lord and his Christ, and he shall reign for ever' (Rev.11.15). We are involved in the strenuous mopping up operation after the victory. Dare we so believe that we show our belief in action with the seriousness that it deserves?

1. *Preparing for Mission in Thamesdown,* Bible Society 1987. Additional unpublished material kindly supplied to the author by Mr George Georgiou, Research Officer.

2. *Faith in the City,* Church House Publishing, 1985, p.xv. Emphasis in the original. The up-date, *Living Faith in the City* reported this despair at the end of 1989. General Synod of the Church of England, 1990, p.vii.

3. ITV 8 April 1991.

4. *The Guardian,* 28 March 1991. *The Poor are Poorer* Statistical Monitoring Unit Department of Social Policy and Social Planning, University of Bristol, 40 Berkeley Square, Bristol.

5. *The Guardian* 24 July 1990.

6. *The Guardian* 8 April 1991.

7. *Living Faith in the City* p.90.

8. *Living Faith in the City* p.103; Peter Townsend and Nick Davidson (eds) *Inequalities in Health* Penguin 1982; Margaret Whitehead, *The Health Divide,* The Health Education Authority, 1987, see especially pp.34f; *Deprivation and Ill-Health,* British Medical Association Board of Science and Education, 1987.

9. Ralf Dahrendorf in *The Guardian,* 1 August 1990.

10. *Christian Aid News* Oct-Dec, 1990.

11. UNICEF: *The State of the World's Children.*

12. James P. Grant, Executive Director of the United Nations Children's Fund, published for UNICEF by Oxford University Press, 1990.

13. J.F. Bethune-Baker, *An Introduction to the early History of Christian Doctrine, Methuen, 1949, pp.81 ff.*

14. *J. Moltmann, The Crucified God,* SCM Press, 1974, pp.178, 176.

15. *J. Moltmann*

16. Lesslie Newbigin, *The Gospel in a Pluralist Society,* SPCK, 1989, p.82).

17.   Julio de Santa Ana in *Youth,* Vol.14 No.1. March 1990, World Council of Churches.

18.   *The Gospel in the Catholic Church,* SPCK, 1990 edition, p.10. For similar sentiments, see also pp.3-5.

19.   David Marquand, *The Unprincipled Society,* Fontana Press, 1988, p.214.

20.   Lesslie Newbigin, *The Open Secret, p.124.*

21.   *The Crucified God,* p.329.

22.   Lesslie Newbigin, *The Open Secret,* Erdmans, 1978, pp.122f.

23.   Moltmann op.cit. pp.322,325.

24.   Peter Marris, *Meaning and Action* second edition, 1987, Routledge and Kegan Paul Ltd. pp.146f.

25.   The project *Kairos Europa — Towards a Europe for Justice* brings together radical grass-roots groups in Europe with this agenda. British representative: Hilary Russell, 23 Garth Drive, Liverpool, L18 6HN.

26.   Lesslie Newbigin, *The Gospel in a Pluralist Society,* SPCK, 1989, pp.198.210.

THE QUIET REVOLUTION
Horace Dammers

The Green Movement for the survival and wellbeing not only of the human family but also of animal and vegetable life in general will fail in its aims unless it is also committed to two objectives; first its integration with the movement for peace and justice within the human family and the more equitable distribution of resources among all its members; and second the global consumption not only of earth-friendly goods and services but also of substantially less of these goods and services by the more affluent. As Gandhi said; 'There is enough in the world for everyone's need but not enough for everyone's greed.' To achieve these aims and objectives nothing less than a revolution is required. But, as I hope to show, it is a revolution without violence, it is a quiet revolution.

Humanity is in debt to the World Council of Churches for championing the aim of 'a just, sustainable and participatory society'. They make the point that justice comes first and many writers and preachers have exposed the centrality of the theme of the justice of God in scripture and in Christian tradition. I need to distinguish three aspects of justice.

First comes God's justice with regard to our eternal salvation. Here, of course, St. Paul is our chief guide. Justification is unequivocally by faith, the loving acceptance of God's free grace. Faith however without works is dead. This subordinate truth is vividly set forth in St. Matthew's Gospel, in for example the story of the judgment of the nations (Mt.25:31-46). Here the criterion of eternal salvation is the giving of drink to the thirsty, the feeding of the hungry, the clothing of the naked, the comforting of the refugee and the visiting of those who are ill or in prison. The second aspect of God's justice is expressed in terms of equitability. God wants all his children, indeed all his creatures to have a fair deal. He abhors the oppression of the poor and the otherwise unjustly oppressed. A third aspect of God's justice concerns the rule of law. The Old Covenant is founded on the revealed law of God, the law which St. Paul, its most acute critic, characterised as 'holy, just and good.' (Rom 7.12). This law went a long way to secure the rights of the poor and protect them from oppression. Therefore law in general must be 'holy, just and good', if it is to reflect God's justice.

In this essay I am mainly concerned with the second aspect of God's justice; a more just and equitable distribution of the Earth's resources, material and spiritual, among the members of the whole human family so that the poor are no longer oppressed. What does a human being need as a minimum in order to enjoy a fully human life and retain his or her human dignity? My list is as follows:—

1. Sufficient clean water for drinking, washing and all basic personal and corporate needs.
2. Sufficiently nutritious and regular food with some variety.
3. A weatherproof home for each family with sufficient privacy.
4. Some changes of clothing.
5. Basic health care for all.
6. Basic education for all, including universal literacy.
7. Sufficient leisure from work for singing or dancing or other entertainment.
8. Appropriate participation in the decisions which affect the individual or community.
9. Adequately paid work for all who can do it. Support from within and outside the family for those who cannot (e.g. children, the aged, the mentally or physically disabled).
10. Freedom to practise and propagate the individual's religious faith and his or her political and other opinions.
11. The rule of law, including the means of changing unjust laws.
12. Freedom from inordinate debt.
13. Freedom from all forms of violence.

It is obvious that this list, thought up on a single solitary walk in the woods, is preliminary and inadequate. Any such list must be for it begs the question as to what meanings should we attach to such words as sufficient, adequate, basic and appropriate? Moreover, justice as a concept involves its extensions, sustainability and participation. Sustainability is an extension of justice. It is justice for future generations, our children, grandchildren and beyond. There would be no value in equitability if it were achieved at the expense of exhausting the Earth's resources and making our planet uninhabitable. Sustainability also secures justice for God's other creatures, animal and vegetable, for whom we have been given a stewardship — a real if limited power to preserve or destroy. Sustainability strikes deep at the roots of our profligacy.

Participation is also an extension of justice. We can consider it under two heads; participation in the good things of life, material and spiritual; and participation in decision making. The sharing out of the good things of life is clearly related to God's justice. But so is participation in decision making. Because of the universality of sin the powerful are always partly at least unjust. So complex systems have to be devised whereby power is shared among the whole people. The larger the unit, the more complex the ideas may have to be. Much work needs to be done to prepare for a truly democratic form of world government. If society is to be truly participatory, the poor and the oppressed must have a proper share in setting the agenda. Many problems would immediately arise. One person might give priority to effective freedom to own land or other property; another might attach importance to a television set in every village. But more positively, participation in decision making increases a person's human dignity and enables him or her to live more responsibly.

As sustainability and participation are both extensions of or even derivatives from justice we should now briefly illustrate at a little more depth this cardinal principle and practice of God's justice. In Jesus' day, as in every other age, before or since, there was massive unemployment and under-employment. There was not nearly enough work to go around. There was massive poverty and social injustice. It was in many ways a cruel world. Jesus told a story about it, one among others — the parable of the Labourers in the Vineyard. (Mt.20.1-16) As day dawns over the Asian village, the landless labourers get up quickly from their sleeping mats. They must be early at the village square if they are to have a share in the limited day labour on which they and their families depend for survival. The village landowner also rises early from his bed, says his prayers, performs his ablutions and eats his breakfast. He is a conscientious man and likes to hire the day labour himself, rather than leave it to a potentially bribable or biased steward. He must in any cae get the men out early into the vineyard to do their best work before the heat of the day. We may presume that he knows them personally, the hard workers and the slackers, those who are getting too old for hard work, those who are weakened by malaria or other disability. He chooses his team and agrees with them a basic wage, the current rate for the job.

He is not only a conscientious employer but also a kindly, generous man. He does not like to think of the 'others standing idle in the market place.' The English word 'idle' in modern usage does not convey the meaning of the original Greek word, 'argous' which simply means 'without work', unemployed, as we say today. There is no suggestion of laziness, as in the English word 'idle'. On the contrary these were the men who did not give up hope, but persisted in hanging about on the offchance of work. In this case their virtue was rewarded. They had no bargaining power, accepting without question the landowner's invitation: 'You go into the vineyard too, and whatever is right I will give you'. This was their only option, the more acceptable in that they knew him to be a just man. He repeated his invitation at mid-morning, midday, mid-afternoon and finally an hour before work stopped for the day.

So what was he going to pay them all, this kindly but locally all-powerful employer? Pro rata, presumably; that would be fair. Those who had worked for only an hour would at least be able to buy a handful of grain or a few vegetables for their children's supper. But no, he deliberately, even provocatively called these last up first and told his steward to pay them a full day's wage. We can imagine their astonishment and delight. And so to them all. As we might expect, those who had done a full day's work complained bitterly. But the owner of the vineyard rightly pointed out that he had fulfilled his contract with them; according to the conditions of the time and place, a fair day's pay for a fair day's work. It was for him to decide if he wished in addition to be generous to the others.

The story as we have it in the gospel ends with a preacher's comment. 'So the last shall be first and the first last'. It looks as if the early Christians spiritualised the story, as they often did with Jesus' stories, applying it in particular to an ecclesiastical question of prime importance to them, and subsequently to us all. Why was God allowing all these rough and ready Gentile Christians to enter His kingdom on equal terms with conscientious Jewish Christians who had worked hard at obeying God's law all their lives? Such an application of the story was, no doubt, fair enough. But if it was legitimate for them to apply the story to their immediately pressing problem, so it is for us, particularly as the story does in fact apply directly to our great contemporary issue of employment, unemployment and under-employment worldwide. What does the story tell us and, equally important, what does it not tell us about God's justice and this particularly challenging form of contemporary oppression?

The story does not tell us about what social and economic structures, capitalist or socialist or mixed or whatever, are best equipped to reduce or even eliminate unemployment and under-employment. To know about that today we have to study the empirical effects of different systems in different places. In this story Jesus does not question the established structure of the all-powerful landowner as the local employer which still obtains in countless villages worldwide today. Nor does the story throw light on any proposals for reducing unemployment put forward by any government or political party. How could it? What the story does is to portray some aspects of God's own way of justice in an unforgettable manner. First the landowner ensures that the work in the vineyard, the process of production if you like, is properly carried out by an adequate labour force. Secondly he negotiates with them collectively a fair wage for the job. Thirdly at his own expense, as the repository of economic power, he makes sure that everyone in the village who is willing and able to work is given work to do, with a sufficient wage for their subsistence. Personally I hope that, when the latecomers arrived on the scene, those who had borne the burden and heat of the day were allowed to slack off a bit; a kind of work sharing. But that's not in the story as we have it. To sum up; efficient production; a sharing of the fruits of that production; a strict honouring of a collectively negotiated contract; and a living wage for all; this latter obtained at the freely given expense of those who could best afford it.

This interpretation of a familiar and authoritative story about the justice of God is coloured by my own, no doubt, superficial observation of Indian village life. The Galilean village in the story is also the global village which we all inhabit. In my book, 'Life Style — A Parable of Sharing' I quoted from a little book called 'Caring for God's World' by Stephen Bayne. The image is so vivid that I shall quote it again:—

'Let us look at the world as if it were a village — a village with a population of 1,000. In this village there would be 140 North and South Americans (60 of them representing the United States); 210 Europeans; 86 Africans; 565 Asians. There would be 300 white people, 700 non-white people, 300 of the 1,000 would be Christians. Half of the total income of the village would be in the hands of the 60 people representing the U.S.A. Almost all the affluent part of the vilage would be composed of Christians from Europe and North America. Over 700 of the 1,000 villagers would be unable to read. Over 500 would be suffering from malnutrition. Over 800 would live in what we call sub-standard housing. No more than 10 would have a university education.'

I have not been able to check Bishop Bayne's figures and indeed I find it hard to believe that seven out of ten human beings are unable to read. If I were from Australia or New Zealand I would like to know where I am to be found in his global village. But there is no doubt that he presents a vivid picture of gross injustice. It is urgently necessary that we should take a leaf out of the landowner's book in Jesus' story. Up to a thousand million fellow members of the human family for whom Christ died and rose again lack the basic necessities that pertain to human dignity. The supply of their emerging needs would provide a rapidly growing market for many of the goods and services which we in the Western world could produce and thus help to solve our own problem of unemployment and underemployment. But first we must help the very poor to secure the necessary purchasing power.

When we consider the complexity and the vast scale of the problems that attend the movement towards a just, sustainable and participatory society we are faced with a broad choice of attitudes, negative or positive. We may be tempted to despair of ever being able to change things. But without hope we can and will do nothing. Hope is essential. This is the positive attitude which leads to revolution. Another word for it, more acceptable to some readers, is repentance; a corporate and personal about turn in the way in which we believe that the necessities of life should be shared.

So what practical way forward can be begin to discern in bringing about change? The theoretical and practical basis of this quiet revolution is to be found in the first of Jesus' beatitudes from the Sermon on the Mount. 'Blessed are the poor in spirit, for theirs is the kingdom of heaven.' (Mt.5.3) When I was first a theological student over forty years ago now, we used to discuss whether this version was to be preferred to that in S.Luke's gospel: 'Blessed are you poor, for yours in the kingdom of God.'

(Lk.6.20) On the one hand it was argued that S.Matthew's version represents a typical spiritualisation of Jesus' own more concrete, down-to-earth and situational teaching. On the other hand it was argued that S.Luke is characteristically indulging his bias towards the poor and so alters the orignal, more generalised statement. Nowadays however biblical scholars in general seem to be more interested in taking the texts as they stand and trying to discern what each writer wanted us to see and to hear. The two versions of the saying may be treated as complementary, not as competing for authenticity. This latter method is more congenial to my present purpose because I believe that the revolution that is now needed is for 'the poor in spirit' to join forces with 'the poor' and so massively change the patterns of production in favour of the latter. By 'the poor in spirit' I mean what I dare to believe Jesus meant; those who identify with the poor not only by taking up their cause but by voluntarily sharing, as he himself did, their lack of riches and the things which riches can buy and, to a greater or lesser extent moderating their demands on the common resources of the earth.

To understand how they are to do this it is necessary to embark on a brief historical excursion. In feudal times political and economic power was concentrated in the hands of the landowning class, with the king at the top of the feudal pyramid. Over the years the rising merchant and capitalist class challenged the feudal powers. It was by combining to withhold their capital from the king and his nobles that they destroyed the divine right of kings, a process which was marked in England by the execution of King Charles I. The landowners stoutly resisted the challenge and a few of them retain to this day considerable wealth and influence, particularly those whose holdings happen to be in the midst of great cities.

By and large the capitalists and merchants retained their political and economic power until in the nineteenth century the workers in turn began to learn the trick of combining to achieve power. They used the same method of withholding or at least threatening to withhold their essential contribution to the common wealth, that is, their labour. By this method they have achieved considerable economic advances in many countries and varying degrees of political power. The power conflict between labour and capital continues to rage in many countries but it is also in the process of being replaced by a new combination at the expense of the universal purchaser of its products. Capitalists increasingly find it convenient to accede to the financial demands of the workers and pass on the consequent price increases to the unfortunate purchasers. The consequence of this continual raising of prices by those who have the power to do so is called inflation. The purchasers of essential goods and services who are hardest hit by this process are neither capitalists nor wage-earners. They include the pensioners, children, the unemployed and a large number of dependent women worldwide.

Each transfer of power, from the landowners to the capitalists, from the capitalists to the workers has only been partial, especially the latter. It is important to emphasise that such transfer as has been achieved, has been achieved by the next aspirants in line combining to withhold their essential contribution to the common wealth. The capitalists combined to refuse to lend money to the king. The workers combined to strike or threaten to strike. Now it is the turn of the purchasers worldwide. 'Purchasers of the world unite! You have nothing to lose but your enslavement to those who persuade you to buy what you neither need nor want.'

At the end of the day the purchasers hold the trump cards. As Adam Smith, prophet of market capitalism, observed: 'The consumer is king.' It has been said that all revolutions start with the bourgeoisie. If a sufficient number of those of us with some surplus purchasing power (including, I suspect, a large majority of the readers of this essay) steadily withhold that purchasing power from the purchase of what we neither need nor want, the whole production process will inevitably turn towards the production of socially useful goods and services, the things that the poor also actually require. It will also become increasingly in the interests of the producers, capitalists and workers alike, that the world's poor should acquire sufficient purchasing power to buy what they will still be producing. With the co-operation of the poor, they will therefore devise new political and economic systems to secure this aim. A just, sustainable and participatory society will be brought into being without the violence that is usually associated with revolution. For who will try to force us at gunpoint to buy cigarettes or whisky or large fast cars or expensive clothes or any other of the thousand and one useless things which clutter up our western society? This, the final major revolutionary transfer of political and economic power — final, because all the members of the human family are basic purchasers — however does require a massive corporate act of repentance. But it is one which, for its fulfilment, can draw on the resources not only of the Christian faith and of other faiths but also of a wide range of humanistic and other benevolent values. In choosing poverty of spirit as the watchword of this revolutionary movement I do not wish to stake an exclusive claim for Christians. The reverse is the case. When Jesus said that the poor in spirit were blessed 'for theirs is the kingdom of heaven', he was addressing the whole human family. The issue is too important for any form of sectarianism.

To achieve our bloodless revolution (and the time is short) we must recruit an active cadre of people, committed both to the aim of a just, sustainable and participatory society and to the revolutionary means to that end — the withholding by a sufficient number of the poor in spirit of their contribution to the production of unnecessary and ecologically destructive goods and services. This has already been started in a small way by such movements as 'The Future in Our Hands', 'Eine Welt', 'The Life Style Movement', and a number of movements of voluntary simplicity in the United States, Australia and elsewhere. Second, we must continue to mount an increasing campaign of education and consciousness raising so that the truth may be universally known about the urgent dangers of the present stage of global injustice, of our unsustainable and ecologically damaging waste of resources and our failure to involve the people in decision making and in the enjoyment of the good things of life. This too is already happening all over the world. Many thousands of the affluent are beginning to realise their responsibilities, many thousands of the oppressed are beginning to realise their prospects of freedom. In our bloodless revolution the affluent must learn to deny themselves what they neither need nor really want and to share with the poor in the decision making as well as in the fruits of production. It is important to emphasise that the end result need not have the characteristics of a dull uniformity. The world's poor on the whole enjoy colour and movement, dance and song, the celebration of festival. They also favour cultural diversity. On the other hand most of the noblest pleasures of richer people in the fields of music, literature and the arts are encouragingly unprofligate of the earth's resources. This movement of education and of consciousness raising is also already taking place through the media and the press, in our schools, churches and other religious bodies, in a number of voluntary agencies and among our political parties.

Next, we must work for a coalition or combination of all the various groups and agencies which are working for a just, sustainable and participatory society. In a small way I know how difficult this is having tried hard to establish just such a combination between the Life Style Movement and the Future in Our hands, two movements that seem to me to have almost identical aims. I have also tried at various times to secure a closer combination between Life Style and various development and conservation agencies but alas, without much success. As in the much greater issue of national sovereignty, it is essential that we learn how to pool our resources and combine our efforts if we are to obtain power, that is the ability to do what we believe has to be done.

We must plan to obtain power, the power to redeem the oppressed and liberate the poor, or rather to assist them decisively to secure their own liberation. The involvement of the poor and oppressed in decision making (democratisation) has to go hand in hand with a widespread moral and spiritual revolution (repentance). The pooling of aspects of national sovereignty has to go hand in hand with the abolition of inordinate debt and the framing of equitable policies of trade and aid. Massive disarmament is congruous with the removal of gross social injustices worldwide which engender violence. The promotion of freedom to practise and propagate one's religious faith fits in with the enhancement of the dignity of the individual.

Most importantly this revolution has to begin with ourselves. Those of us whose income (after the deduction of taxes and of whatever we already give away to charity) exceeds the national per capita income must at least ensure that we do not spend annually more than the national average. If we wish to show a greater solidarity with the poor we may choose to select a lower figure. Whatever income is surplus to this voluntary limitation on our spending will be available to us either to give away; or to save (e.g. to provide for the future security of dependents); or to pay off the capital of any debts we may have incurred before entering into this commitment.

I began with a slogan derived from the World Council of Churches. I end with another. The three aims of 'justice, peace and integrity of creation' are complementary and mutually essential to each other. Ready to hand for their achievement by means of the Quiet Revolution is the burgeoning Green Movement. The 'Greens' are already prominent in the recruitment of a cadre of people personally committed to a more equitable distribution of the Earth's resources among the whole human family and to the conservation and development of those resources in such a way that this human family may live harmoniously with other forms of life. They are already committed to a considerable campaign of education and consciousness raising. And they are seeking to obtain the power to implement some of the steps that have to be taken towards the Quiet Revolution. For the reader to 'live green' is his or her personal step towards this Quiet Revolution, an idea whose time has come, an idea with decisive survival value for humans and for other creatures, an idea therefore which will prevail. The future of the Green Movement as a major contributor to the advancement of the Quiet Revolution depends on its ability to hold together in a creative balance the complementary values of peace and justice alongside the value of the integrity of creation.

Section Four

Section Four focuses on issues of sexuality and human personhood. Both Una Kroll and Rowan Williams direct their concern towards the Church's attitude towards homosexuals and the material with which they are dealing arises out of the debate which took place in the Church of England's General Synod during November 1987. The debate and its conclusions marked a low point in the Synod's life and its consequences have been far-reaching for homosexuals generally and for homosexual clergy in particular. But all Christians have been diminished by the dishonesty, cowardice, mis-information and prejudice which surfaced so starkly in 1987 and to which we have all been heirs since. The essays by Una Kroll and Rowan Williams were first presented as lectures at a conference organised in Bristol on Christianity and Homosexuality on October 14th 1989. The conference was itself an attempt to consider the issue of homosexuality more honestly, realistically and compassionately than had taken place during the last two years. These two essays are included to honour Paul's commitment to the right of homosexuals to receive equal rights and respect within the church and in society. Although he died before the Bristol conference took place, he supported their rights vigorously as a member of the General Synod and engaged in a great deal of personal pastoral care amongst homosexuals around the time of the Synod debate. The final short essay is included to honour Paul's concern with the issue of women in the church and the process of debate surrounding the ordination of women to the priesthood — issues which had a profound effect upon Paul's whole understanding of the way in which issues of justice and peace are inter-linked.

Misandry and Misogyny in the context of Homophobia and Heterophobia

Una Kroll

First presented as a lecture at a conference organised in Bristol on Christianity and Homosexuality on October 14th 1989.

I had intended to address myself only to an examination of the roots of misandry, the hatred of men, and misogyny, the hatred of women, but I have come to realise that fear of homosexuals has certain important consequences in relation to man-woman relationships so that if I am to understand misandry and misogyny I must first examine the roots of homophobia and its opposite, heterophobia, for fear and hate are closely linked with each other. Our task as Christians is to work with God to overcome these evils and if we are to do that work we shall have to make sure that we ourselves are not overcome by the very evils that we are seeking to eliminate from Church and society.

The terms homophobia and heterophobia are well known. Fear of homosexuals and heterosexuals occurs in all societies and it fuels hatred and persecution of individuals and groups. That much is obvious: less obvious is what is meant by the word, "fear" so I just want to spell out my own understanding of the way in which I am using this word in the context of this essay.

"The fear of the Lord is the beginning of wisdom." (Ps 111:10). Fear in that context alludes to awe, the kind of awe that makes us pay attention to God in such a way that we learn to be obedient to God's laws. There are many allusions to this kind of "fear" in the Bible, for example:
"Work out your salvation with fear and trembling." (Phil 2:12)
"They were all gathered together, walking in the fear of the Lord." (Acts 9:31)

"Fear", — awe, reverence, obedience, is one way of using the word, "phobia" but I am not using it in this way: nor am I using it to describe healthy fear. It would, for instance, be entirely proper to be afraid of a green mamba snake if it reared up in your way and to want to shun its company, or even to kill it lest it kill you. No, I am using "phobia" to describe a persistent, irrational or abnormal attitude, be it intellectual, emotional or spiritual, which prompts one created being to shun another. So, for instance, we speak about being unusually afraid of spiders, dogs and confined spaces as arachnophobia, canophobia and claustrophobia. Our fears incline us to avoid contact with spiders, dogs, or enclosed small spaces as the case may be. Phobias often start from an instance where fear has been an entirely proper response to an unpleasant experience. So, for instance, one child whose mother screamed with fear when she saw a tarantula on its bed, may develop a fear of all spiders, not just the one that could have killed her. Another child who had been bitten by a dog might develop a fear of all dogs, not just the one who inflicted pain. Yet another child who had been shut in an elevator for a time might develop a fear of all elevators or closed-in spaces. A fear that began as a rational proper fear becomes, for reasons we do not yet fully understand, an irrational, general fear that cannot be controlled. Phobias do not always start from the time of the incident that provoked fear. They may begin much later, even as late as adult life, when some circumstance may break down the strong defence that has hitherto enabled someone to cope with a severe fear in public, or when a repressed fear suddenly surfaces and becomes overwhelming. These phobias are very unpleasant and quite often handicapping. I can recall, for instance, a Reverend Mother who was terrified of all spiders. Until she had been treated for her phobia she was unable to visit her Sisters in countries where spiders were always around the house. I have known adults unable to visit friends who have dogs and one of my friends has to walk up the stairs in high rise buildings because she cannot face using the lifts.

Phobias, then, are potentially handicapping conditions. Moreover, we are often ashamed of them and may try to conceal them, even from ourselves. Alternatively we may defend them vigorously by justifying them or rationalising them. We find all kinds of excuses to avoid the object of our fear, the zoo, the neighbour's dog, the high rise elevator. "It's not right to lock up animals", we say, or, "I never go to the zoo; it's too expensive", or, "dogs give you nasty diseases, like blindness", or, "high rise buildings destroy family life; they all ought to be pulled down."

A consideration of these issues is germane to homophobia and heterophobia because they like any other phobias are pathological conditions *and* they are handicapping. Once well established they are not fully under our control and we will need help to overcome them for they do not yield easily to rational argument, persuasion or forceful exposure to the object of fear.

These phobias towards members of the same species, who differ from us in certain specific ways, are widespread in western society and they are common. They can affect *all* of us whatever our sexual orientation, even though homophobia is a more commonly recognised attitude than heterophobia. One way of dealing with our fears is by rationalisation which involves, as we have already noted, assigning value to our phobic behaviour. We do exactly the same, only with greater vigour, when we find ourselves wanting to shun homosexuals or heterosexuals because we are afraid of them. That statement is rather too general for my liking so let me unpack it a bit by considering some of the major roots of homophobia as I see it from the perspective of a counsellor who is also reasonably well read on the issues under consideration.

Women and men, of either gender or of any sexual orientation, may become homophobic:

a) *because of a bad experience, usually in early childhood.*

The easiest example to take is that of a boy who has been painfully buggered at an early age. The shock and pain may have been "forgotten" but the buried memory causes him to shudder at the thought of buggery and as he cannot envisage any other way of sexual intimacy between same-sex couples he remains afraid of homosexuals.

A less dramatic example might be that of a teenage girl who fell in love with a man she did not know to be "gay". When rejected by him she was affronted, not only by the fact that she was not sexually attractive to him, but also because she had not recognised the signs of his homosexuality. Rejection and hurt pride easily transmute into the kind of fear that prompts a woman to avoid contact with known homosexuals.

b) *because of conditioning.*

We are all socially conditioned from birth. Our family milieu is an important determining factor in our attitudes towards sexuality. If you had the kind of family in which "poofs" and "dykes" were despised and feared you will necessarily find your subconscious mind cluttered up with the same kind of mixed fear/hate fantasies and they will condition your attitudes towards people of homosexual orientation. Depending upon the length of exposure and your own vulnerability to the people who hold such views you will emerge either conditioned to homophobia, or have a massive reaction to the conditioning which may result in some ambivalence towards your own gender identity and sexuality and to a certain degree of insecurity that can lead to over-defensiveness of your own position.

c) *because of uncertaintity about your own sexuality.*

When people know who they are, what kinds of relationships they enjoy and what kinds of sexual appetites they have they will be secure in their gender and orientation identity. If, however, they are still in the formative stage, or are feeling insecure, they often try to adopt one disposition unequivocally, in an attempt to identify with the kind of person they think they want to be. Someone who is doing this consciously or, more usually, unconsciously may tend to become fearful if other people relate to them as if they were the kind of person they most definitely have not chosen to be.

d) *because of a general fear of all sexuality.*

This is sometimes bolstered by a religious conviction that chastity (celibacy) is "perfect" and that all other forms of sexul relationship "fall short" of this ideal in varying ways.

Christians who belong to main stream institutional churches are particularly vulnerable to his kind of fear, both because of Biblical literalism and because Christian leaders, unlike their Master, Jesus Christ, are afraid to associate with unpopular causes of any kind.

e) *because of associated fears.*

The excessive homophobia we have all witnessed since the mid 1980's has been due largely to a resurgence of the suppressed or repressed fears about homosexuality which have surfaced as a result of its association in peoples' minds with the disease commonly known as A.I.D.S.

f) *because of false value assignations to heterosexuality.*

Heterosexuality, being a more common condition than homosexuality, is generally regarded as the normative way of life, seeing that one of it's purposes is the safeguarding of the human species through procreation. It, therefore, attracts the label "good" because normative and all other forms of sexuality are "less good" or downright "bad", because they are not. Those who are homosexuals, particularly those whose homosexuality is unrecognised, can become afraid of the consequences of the "bad" label even though they are not afraid of being homosexual or ashamed of it.

It would be a mistake to think that only heterosexual people are homophobic. Many homosexuals are infected with the condition and some become ill because of it.

Heterosexuals can be feared for any of the reasons applicable to homosexuals, but in reverse as it were. In addition it can occur:

a) *when heterosexuals oppress homosexuals and others.*

90

Oppressed people of any kind tend to resent/fear/hate those who rule them, exploit them or ignore their very existence. If, then, perchance the oppressed get free they sometimes can be as ruthless and cruel towards people in their power as their own oppressors once were to them. I have to say that I have seen this kind of factor operate very unkindly in regard to women. *Some* homosexual priests appear to have an almost pathological hatred of women whom they delight in oppressing. It is as if, being unable to be dominant over the world of "macho" men they *have* to dominate women simply in order to show their superiority towards those whom they regard as needing to be kept in their place, kept inferior. In saying this I am **not** alluding specifically to the matter of women priests but to a more generalised experience of women in the Church.

b)   *because society is patriarchially organised at present.*

Patriarchy and hierarchy seem to me to be bedfellows, with white heterosexual men being seen to be most "good", dominant, responsible, and fit to rule and black homosexual women as most "bad", inferior, irresponsible and unfit to rule. In order to maintain this dominance, heterosexuals sometimes resort to violence to intimidate those whom they systematically oppress. They lynch or castrate homosexuals: they rape women. They will sometimes go so far as to bugger men and women as an act of violence rather than as an expression of love. Small wonder then that some people who have been the victims of such violence, or who have heard about it, find themselves heterophobic because the fear of one kind of individual has extended itself to all of that orientation. But, however understandable, heterophobia is as much of a disease process as homophobia. Fear can transform itself into hatred which can in its turn oppress, maim or otherwise destroy any individual who is unfortunate enough to become weak enough for the heterophobic person to overpower.

In my experience these phobias are common. They also translate easily into anger. If you watch a mother who sees her child run out into the road without due care and in consequence nearly gets run over by an on-coming vehicle you will see what I mean. The mother's terrible fear often changes into undue anger with the child for having been careless in crossing the road. The poor child is already frightened by the experience: to this may be added the angry voice, harsh words and even slaps of his or her distraught mother.

It would be an over-simplification to think that misogyny and misandry have their roots wholly in homophobia and heterophobia, but I do believe that sexual phobias of the kinds I have listed are an important contributory factor to the development of misogyny and misandry.

Frankly I am puzzled by these two conditions. I know that they often **do** have the same genesis as homophobia and heterophobia, but I feel that there are more roots to be discovered than the ones I can see. I can understand why some women are afraid of and hate some men and I can understand why some men are afraid of and hate some women. I cannot so easily understand why some men and women hate other men and women as intensely and collectively as they appear to do. Men certainly are no more immune than women from being afraid of and hating their own sex, especially if there is an "otherness" about the hated person that justifies the hate. Thus homosexual males can hate heterosexual males and heterosexual males can hate homosexual males because they are afraid of being identified with them and thus having to share their "badness" in the sight of God and Man. There is a kind of "pecking order" which operates in all human communities whereby the "top" people oppress those below them in the pecking order and keep them in their place. Because of the peculiar mating behaviour that exists in Western society I can also understand why heterosexual females can be afraid of and hate their sisters who are also their rivals for a mate's affections. What I find far harder to understand, however, is why homosexual men and lesbians can be misogynists and why lesbians and homosexual men can be misandrists. They are, after all, all at the bottom of the pile, all oppressed, all discriminated against in society and I would have expected them to find solidarity with each other in a very creative way.

You and I who belong to Christ's body know that we live in a kind of society where homophobia, heterophobia, misogyny and misandry are commonplace. We are ourselves inescapably part of that society, both as oppressed people and as oppressors of others. We also know that we belong to a God who does not hate us, for whoever we are and whatever our dispositions we are loved by God indiscriminately. Because we know that we are loved by God we can learn to love ourselves and others as ourselves. We are, indeed, called to that stance by Christ Himself:

> "They are not of the world, even as I am not of the world. Sanctify them in the truth; thy word is truth."   (John 17:16-17)

> "You are all one in Christ Jesus."   (Gal 3:28)

> "For this is the message which you have heard from the beginning, that we should love one another."   (1 John 3:11)

> "Love your enemies and pray for those who persecute you."   (Matt 5:44)

Can anything be clearer? No, it cannot. Yet, we all know that our Churches are plagued with the evils of homophobia, heterophobia, misandry and misogyny. We also know that this happens because we are sinners and that we can have no hope of redemption from those sins except through Christ who alone can give us the grace to vanquish fear and overcome sin.

"Perfect love casts out fear." (1 John 4:18)

None of us loves perfectly, but I think we **do** want to love as well as we possibly can and we **do** trust God to give us grace according to our need. What then can we do about these sad evils which cause so much misery to so many people, ourselves included? Those of us who, in our several ways, have been the victims of these terrible phobias and hates must ask ourselves some questions. What can we do with them? How can we help those who oppress us to develop more creative attitudes towards us? How can we help our brothers and sisters who are oppressed to resist the damaging and draining loss of self-confidence and self-esteem that so often seems to happen when individuals and social agencies in the community denigrate and oppress them?

Here are a few suggestions:

1) We can take a good long look at our own attitudes towards each other and if we find ourselves prejudiced in any way we can begin to make amends, even if slowly and painfully. We should never be afraid of our own fears, but acknowledge them and help God to help us to overcome them.

2) We can belong to and/or support small groups of people who want to develop their self-confidence and self-esteem by sharing experiences and thoughts.

3) We can do all we can to help people to develop more positive attitudes towards sexuality, sexual orientation and sexual behaviour. This will generally be slow work, needing much patience and repetition in a persevering kind of a way.

4) We can actively seek the company of those who are shunned by others. This is costly for we will share their unpopularity and be discriminated against as well.

5) We can actively seek the company of our 'enemies' and not shun them either in prayer or in Church, even if they do make us feel unpleasantly afraid or angry. To do this kind of work we will need to become quite self-aware and able to be ourselves in every situation rather than becoming travesties of ourselves, even if that does seem expedient for the sake of long term gain.

And it is with this last point that I shall draw to a conclusion for in all of this, I speak as one who has a lot of experience of the interior twisting that can go on when you are seduced into remaining 'silent' for the sake of peace, or into making concessions in negotiations for the sake of the 'weaker brethren." Concessions there must sometimes be, that I know, but concessions can only be made if they nevertheless preserve the integrity of both parties to the concession. The vote taken in the General Synod in November 1987 when homosexuality was bracketed with adultery as a sin, showed just how difficult it is to maintain the integrity of one's views on any controversial issue without totally compromising oneself. The point at issue was surely this. No practising Christian homosexual would voluntarily enter into a partnership of love if he or she thought that love to be sinful, yet, during that debate I saw many of my 'gay' friends voting for the Bishop of Gloucester's amendment because they thought it was at least less condemnatory than Tony Highton's original motion. But was it? For it demanded that, far from affirming our homosexual brothers and sisters right to give and receive love, we were forced to accede in an interpretation of that love which denied both their integrity and our own. I would not support homosexual friends in the way I do if I thought that same-sex love was sinful. I do not see either the love or the expression of that love to be sinful for I believe that sexual acts can be an expression of God's love inasmuch as they are an expression of mutual love and a desire for permanency in companionship, whether or not that is accomplished until death parts us asunder. To have voted otherwise would have been to deny all that I believe in about the way in which homophobia can and must be overcome and the way in which loving relationships can and must be affirmed, if we in the Church are to reflect something essential about the inclusive love of God.

The Sexuality of the Pastor

Rowan Williams

First presented as a lecture at a conference organised in Bristol on Christianity and Homosexuality on October 14th 1989.

I want to begin with a Bible story. It is a familiar one, but I'd like you to hear it in a new context. Zacchaeus was sitting on a branch of a tree and wondering how he came to be there. He was saying to himself rather bitterly that there was after all no inconspicuous way of climbing trees; which was why there were little boys dancing round the foot of the tree, pointing up at him, and why a certain amount of rotten fruit was adhering to his person; but it seemed worth it and he knew that when the real crowds arrived, their attention would be on someone else. And so it was: when the little group came in sight approaching the gates of the town, people stopped worrying about him and started looking for the stranger who was visiting. Because Zacchaeus was beginning to relax a little bit (as far as he could relax with the branch of the sycamore tree sticking into his bottom) he thought, I am probably safe now; I can watch. So it was a very bad moment when the little group in the middle distance stopped, and the figure in the middle waves, and about nine hundred and forty-three pairs of eyes suddenly turned round in the direction in which the stranger was waving and a voice was shouting something across the crowds. "Oh God" said Zacchaeus "it's me!". The voice was shouting "Zacchaeus". A silence fell on the crowd, and Zacchaeus heard the voice shouting across the distance, "I want to have dinner with you". There was a long pause. The eyes still looked curiously up at the sycamore tree. Zacchaeus slipped down and the crowds parted before him like water. He went up to the stranger and the stranger said "I want to have dinner with you". And he put out his hand and he touched Zacchaeus' cheek. Zacchaeus said, stupidly, "I feel I ought to do something before you come and have dinner. What if I gave some money away?"

"We'll talk about that later" said the stranger and squeezed his shoulder.

Zacchaeus stumbled along in a daze in the wake of the little group, part of his

95

mind thinking, just how many people will there be at the front door tomorrow morning wanting their money back? And part of his mind thinking how long is it since anyone called me 'Zacchaeus' as opposed to 'that bloody tax inspector' or 'that bloody collaborator'? And another part of his mind thought, how long is it since anyone has touched me with love? And it seemed worthwhile.

How do we hear the good news? What is it like to hear the gospel? Hearing good news is knowing we are wanted; and that perhaps is the most fundamental and the simplest fact the Christian gospel has to convey to human beings — that they are wanted and that they are wanted really rather urgently by God, so urgently that there is nothing particular that He is going to ask them to do first. He just wants them as they are.

That wanting will in due course mould and change the lives of those who are wanted, as all love must. Christian ethics is about charting some of the ways in which that pressure works — Zacchaeus' conversion to sharing his money, the adulterous woman's presumed conversion to faithfulness. These are patterns to be discerned, disciplines to be created. But I want to speak here **not** about ethics but about what comes **before** ethics in Christianity, and makes ethics possible — the reaching out of God to us.

What is it then that is required of a minister of the Christian good news? I should say that the **first thing** is that they must have heard the good news, that they must know that they are wanted; which is why I started with the story of Zacchaeus — the story about an outsider who knew he was wanted. Because he knew he was wanted he was able himself to want the love and fellowship of others. Very recently a minister of the Christian gospel told me that only when she knew she was loved by another human being had her ministry come to mean anything whatsoever, and that for several years she felt she had known **nothing** of God whatsoever in her ministry. This is fundamental and very simple; but that is the way it is. To preach the Christian good news is to have heard it first, and to make your life a way of communicating good news — that is of communicating the welcome with which you have been welcomed. That is the primary responsibility of the minister of the Christian gospel. It is also of course the responsibility of **anyone** who is a Christian, because we are all preachers of the gospel; but we are asking something of ministers in particular, asking them, presumably, to show us what it is like to be a Christian in a slightly more exposed way than most of us. But more of that later.

When in the Ordinal of the Church of England we find the requirement that the ordinand should frame his or her life and that of their household to the doctrine of Christ and be wholesome and good examples to the flock, I take it that the 'doctrine' that is in question is above all the good news of being wanted by God, because that is the 'doctrina' of Christ — what Christ **teaches.** Now, for the vast majority of the human race, understanding that you are wanted is an experience that does not come all in one lump and simply from one source. It depends on all kinds of things. It can depend upon a shattering unexpected experience of God; it can depend on something like Zacchaeus' story; it can depend on something like a story which is told by St. Teresa in her autobiography. She describes there her early years as a nun, years in which she thought for a bit that she was doing quite well, and then, because she thought she was doing quite well, she did not really think about how she was doing at all. She got used to being a nun with a decent reputation for piety and holiness; whom people occasionally came to see and ask advice from; but she knew quite well at one level that nothing much was going on in her. She was more or less 'dead' for nearly twenty years as a nun, and she tells us that the experience that made a difference to her was that one day she was confronted, as if for the first time, by an image in the cloister of the suffering Christ. What she thought that image conveyed to her was not what it might be expected to convey — guilt that she made Him suffer — but rather, how much he must **need** her. Her response was, He is so lonely, He might even need me.

From there on, there grows in her that sense of being urgently, desperately wanted by God, which is the root of everything else Teresa does. Her whole sense of what the Christian community life is about, as she sets it out in her great book, "The Way of Perfection", is very largely about how on earth we communicate in our Christian lives the **wanting of God.** Now, for the vast majority of us, being wanted has to do with sexuality. It is about the affirmation of acceptance, the 'yes' saying to the whole of us, not bits and pieces, but body and soul together — if you can draw that distinction at all. For most of us, to know we are loved and wanted means that somewhere we need to learn we are wanted in our bodies — that we are wanted in our wholeness.

As I have suggested, there are those like Teresa who, in consecrated celibacy, learn this in other ways — although I very much doubt whether such people ever learn it without **some** knowledge of what it is like to be wanted in their bodies. What all this is working up to is simply that the Christian minister, the minister of the Christian good news needs to be a person who knows him or herself to be wanted in their wholeness, to be affirmed and welcomed as a body. This is where we need to start thinking about the sexuality of the pastor; and about the damage that is done by not understanding that ministers of the Christian gospel can only minister the Christian gospel if they know something about human need — **their** human need. We do not always think very much about that, at least, clergy probably **do,** although they tend not to talk about it. And that is where the difficult questions arise about those whose sexuality does not correspond very easily to what we have generally taken for granted (The Norm).

It seems to me that, for example, the homosexual clergy person, male or female, needs to be, like anyone else, a person loved, affirmed and welcomed in their bodiliness; and unless you assume the rather curious statistical myth that the vocation to celibacy is fantastically higher, proportionally, among the homosexual than the heterosexual population (which is what a good many people appear to take for granted), then you have to assume that such persons require the affirmation of loving sexually and being loved sexually. Something of the same arises in the context of discussing divorced clergy. I want to say a word or two about clerical marriages in this connection. The cleric whose marriage has come apart, the cleric who is struggling with a decaying marriage is **no less in need** of being wanted; and that includes being sexually wanted. How are we going to deal with that without acknowledging that such a person has a reasonable and **christian** claim for that need to be met? It isn't a matter of demanding 'rights' to sexual satisfaction, or of supposing that any immediate solution is obvious; simply of recognizing that the problem here is one that is really bound up with how the gospel is preached.

That is almost all that I have got to say. However I would like to touch briefly on some of the questions that arise in the wake of this rather elementary introduction. What, for instance, are we going to do with the notion of the minister as exemplary, as a wholesome example to the flock of Christ? It seems to me that here we are asking about the **symbolism** of certain sorts of lives — what **meanings** are communicated by certain kinds of life. And this means asking what is communicated by the life of a Christian minister who is sexually frustrated at a fundamental level, or by the life of a Christian minister who is involved in a decaying and destructive marriage. We are told that it is very important that the standards of marriage should be upheld by the Church and its ministers. I agree; but the question is how those standards are conceivably upheld by marriages that are manifestly destructive of the human beings involved, and what, pastorally and evangelically, such relationships convey. Leaving aside for the time being all the questions we like to leap in to asking about praise and blame, innocence and guilt, in all this, what do we actually do when the family life of a minister is a sign of death rather than life? And what do we do when the life and lifestyle of a minister is pervaded by concealment, anxiety or shame? What do we do when the life of a minister is lived under the shadow of a deep division between the private and the public, when what is most important in a minister's life cannot be allowed in any way publically to nourish or uphold the ministry that is being exercised? What does that say?

This is the situation in which a great deal of the Church has caught itself. It means that, for some Christian ministers, what helps most profoundly to make the gospel immediate to them, in terms of the faithful, costly wanting of them and promise to them of another person, cannot be acknowledged in their own communicating of the gospel, because of the secrecy and fear surrounding the whole area of homosexuality. If we are discussing the sexuality of the pastor and the pastor, requiring like anyone else, to know that he or she is wanted, then we are talking about how the Church lets itself be ministered to as well. But if we are looking also at the whole issue of **example** then we must face the reality of **evil** example and **destructive** example — death-giving example, the example of death-giving relationships among ministers, and the deathliness of secrecy and fear. We must not ask anyone to be an example to us of contempt or disregard of the real needs of human beings. We must not ask anyone to be an example to us of corrupting silence and fear. We must not ask of our ministers what in fact distorts the gospel.

Well then, do clergy in some sense stand under different standards of judgement from the rest of the church? Only in one sense and I think it is this -- I mentioned earlier that the minister of the gospel has the responsibilty to hear the gospel, and, in his or her life, to turn it into communication. So surely what we are asking clergy to take responsibility for is how their needs or their flaws, their vulnerability and their humanity in general, are to be turned into preaching. **That** is the standard by which a minister of the gospel surely is to be judged — not whether such a person is keeping lots of rules satisfactorily, not whether such a person is successfully managing their lives in every respect, but whether those **unmanageable** factors in a human life, those factors which have to do with vulnerability and uncertainty, which have to do often with tragedy and fragmentation, are becoming the material of bringing good news. That is the responsibility of the minister, that is the standard of judgement. And once again it is not something different in **kind** from that for which all Christians are responsible.

If we suppose that it is somehow acceptable for divorced people or homosexual people to be baptised and communicant members of the church, I find it very hard to see why we should not suppose that they are acceptable holders of public ministerial office in the church. I think if we suggest that there **is** a distinction there, we are falling back into the old 'counsels-and-precepts' idea that so damaged the life of the church for such a long time — general bits of advice, 'standing orders' for all Christian people on the one hand, and then the fast stream, the Honours class, that does the celibacy option. I do not think that this will quite do. I do not think that it will do either to suggest that, within the church, there are those on whom the requirements of meeting some supposed norm of sexual behaviour weighs more heavily than others. How can that not issue in some sort of dishonesty? No: we need to see that it is human vulnerability and neediness that most powerfully express the transcendence, the beauty, the glory and the disturbingness of God.

Think about **saints;** about those who have made the gospel concrete in our lives and our age. I remember in San Francisco, a couple of years ago, when I was at a conference there, seeing an ikon of Martin Luther King carried in procession. I suspect he would have hated it — just as I suspect John Bunyan would have hated having a Feast Day in the Church of England! But as I looked at that ikon I thought uncomfortable thoughts about how King would rate in the conventional morality stakes. The FBI were delighted with his compulsive sexual adventuring; it is a paradoxical part of his moral stature that he never let himself be blackmailed into silence. He knew he was, in his private life, a needy and confused man, and offered no justification or excuse. I defy anyone to say that his is not a life that adds up to a word of gospel to our century. We can set alongside the various things that King might have got wrong or the various ways in which he does not live up to the standards we might like someone to live up to, the fact that he is one of the few human beings in our century who has actually made an identifiable, perceptible change in the western world's advance towards something faintly resembling justice, and done it in the name of Jesus Christ and in the power of the Holy Spirit.

Or again: Gonville French-Beytagh, former Dean of Johannesburg, makes it very clear in his autobiography that his own life before and after ordination was not one which would wholly commend itself to certain styles of clerical ethics. But that life, in its witness in South African, and I think also in its more unobtrusive but wonderful witness since, was a life that 'adds up' in the same way. I owe Gonville a great deal for my own soul, partly, quite simply, because the witness of his books and of his preaching has been the witness of a man who heard good news in the very fibre of his being.

Then a much less known figure, but one who equally fleshes out the gospel, the Russian nun, Mother Maria Skobtsova, who was executed in Ravensbruck at the very end of the Second World War, having (so the story goes) grown up in a Russian landowning family at the turn of the century, and been heavily involved in the cultural, moral and political turmoil of the age. She was twice divorced. She substituted herself for another prisoner on the way to the gas chamber. Mother Maria was not what you would call a conventional Russian Orthodox nun. She had a dramatic past, certainly did not live an ordinary 'nunnish' life in Paris, where she devoted most of the 1930's to helping refugees, and, eventually, to helping Jews in particular. (It was her confessor, Father Dimitri, who when interrogated by the Gestapo about his Jewish friends, held up the Crucifix on his breast and said "Have you met his Jew?" That was Mother Maria's theology.) She is one of the most extraordinary transformative figures of those dark years, along with people like Bonhoeffer and others better known than her. But it is not a **conventional** life; it is a life flawed, marked by need and ambiguity; **and** it is a life of holiness — it 'adds up' to the gospel. Well, if that is what we are asking for, if we are asking for sanctity rather than heroism, and if we can be clear about what we mean by sanctity as we look at people like these, we may perhaps come back to the whole question of what we expect of our pastors in a slightly new light. We may be able to challenge the really **deeply** damaging myths about heroism, about the need for a pastor to 'get it right'. We may be able to move that small step further toward the possibility of a Christian minister being honest about his or her sexuality; of looking in this light at the whole question of divorce and remarriage for the clergy; of looking in this light at the question of the homosexual cleric, male or female. The **first** thing to remember is that the 'example' which matters is of a life in which good news has been heard.

So I hope I may have opened one or two doors into thinking these matters through further; I'm sure I will have caused disappointment in having absolutely no practical solutions to offer — but then that is one of the things that professors notoriously cannot do.

Reflections on The Psychology
of a Male Priesthood

Sue Walrond-Skinner

There is a sense in which the subject matter of this short essay should have come earlier in this collection because the refusal of the Church of England to ordain women as priests was a crucial and early learning experience for Paul in his relationship with the institutional Church. As for many others, it was his experiences at theological college that presented Paul for the first time with a small, excluded and vociferously hurting group of people for whom the Church had nothing to offer. During his time as college, some of these women left the course, unable to see any hope for a full acceptance of themselves as persons. Others struggled to change a dominant college community culture and learned much in the process of how things were going to be for us when we emerged to work in the community of the Church.

It was typical of Paul that as he began to recognise that these women were claiming a share of God's justice — not primarily for themselves but on behalf of all women — he quickly identified with their pain, despite his previous strongly held evangelical views about the relationship of women and men. He became part of the debate, part of the struggle and part of the solution in seeking a way forward towards radical change. For what was different and typical of Paul's involvement in the women's issue was that, as usual, he felt it as a call to personal, prophetic action, not simply as a call to debate and solidarity of a less personally involving kind.

Thus it was that he took the decision, sometime towards the end of his period at theological college, that he would not be ordained until women could also be admitted to priestly orders. His decisions had immediate personal consequences for him because the job market in the Church for such a person was restricted. Paul was unemployed for 6 months until he finally found a Bishop who would licence him and a parish who would accept him simply as a lay worker — a designation he retained until he died.

This new understanding and new solidarity with the issue of women's ordination marked a profound turning point in Paul's life. For as for all of us, Paul's learning was still only partial in this matter and one of the tragedies of his short life was that he had really only just begun to travel a much more personal journey, which was leading him to understand and to integrate the many rich and varied aspects of his own personality.

Just as Paul pursued his personal explorations alongside his political commitments, so it is helpful for us all to gain some clearer understanding of the psychological referents which underpin the two major arguments against the ordination of women. We will consider some ideas from the theories of dependency in developmental psychology, sexual stereo-typing, systemic inter-dependence and crisis theory and allude briefly to the concept of reflexivity as it applies to any argument in which one is personally involved. We will use these ideas to try and gain a better understanding of both the process and the content of the two main arguments advanced against the ordination of women and to understand why, on the contrary, it is necessary, for the psychological health of both women and men, to proceed as quickly as possible to the ordination of women as priests.

There are two major arguments against the ordination of women as priests, which are I believe fundamental to every subsidiary argument or pragmatic consideration. The first is the initator/receiver argument, whereby the masculine and the feminine are linked respectively with the initiation and the response to or reception of that which has been initiated. From this is derived the argument of masculine priestly **headship**. The second is the normative argument, whereby the masculine is viewed as the normative mode of humanity, against which femininity is compared. From this follows the argument of masculine priestly **representation**. Both arguments are however reducible ultimately to a single core belief — that is that the feminine is in some sense defective, inferior or secondary to the male and is therefore inadequate and unsuitable as a vehicle for representing God, leading his people or mediating Holy things.

Both arguments are based upon some selective use of developmental psychology, of work done on sexual stereo-typing and (in the second case) on analytical psychology, and despite the work of those who support the ordination of women to the priesthood the arguments have changed very little over the last two decades. This is perhaps not surprising because psychology is not a discipline which the writer can get wholly outside — it is a reflexive activity in the Kellian sense, and it is inevitable that we are all influenced in our arguments by the very psychological processes that we are seeking to describe. (Kelly 1955) Thus the more the psychological arguments **for** the ordination of women are advanced, the more resistant (because under threat) do its opponents become. And the more that the psychological arguments **against** the ordination of women are counter-advanced, the more resistant (because under threat) do its proponents become. The relationship between the two view points is in some measure systemic and circular and thus leads to certain consequences:—

1.   There is no beginning and no end to the argument.

2.   Each side becomes more entrenched in their view point because they are progressively more threatened by the other.

3.   "More of the same" arguments leads to sameness not difference.

4.   Only difference (or variety in systems terms) can lead to a way out of the impasse.

We cannot, by definition do much more than "bear in mind" our reflexive involvement in the systemic processes of the argument in which we are embedded — but that "bearing in mind" can sometimes serve to reduce the hostility and help us to value the arguments of our opponents as the necessary shadow side of our own. Such reflective valuing of the opponent's argument should not however lead us to blur the sharpness of our own. Rather, this reflection on process may lead us to greater clarity in understanding both our own and the other and the relationship between them.

To return to the content of the first argument against the ordination of women. Inherently men are viewed as the initiators, women the receivers within any action. The argument is traced from biology and from the act of sexual intercourse and has two aspects. Physically the male "initiates" the act of sexual intercourse and he "gives" through his penis the semen to the female. The female "responds" to the male's initiation and she "receives" the gift of his sperm. From this argument is deduced the fact that men are inherently the initiators and the prime movers of all action, change and growth and they are thereby endowed with qualities of altruism that enable them to reach out to the female. (The argument is sometimes framed within the idea of the male as the "source" of activity and initiative rather than the "prime mover" but the development of the argument is the same). The male is able, because of his primacy in the creation to be altruistic i.e. to have regard for somebody else. By the same token he is the natural leader of the other because he is the head and the source of the other's being. The arguments advanced by the Church over the years for the headship of man over woman and her necessary submission to this state of affairs are well summarised by Furlong (1991 pp 33-40). They are restated as a descriptive "given" from the Genesis story in the statement by the House of Bishop's, Issues in Human Sexuality (1991):

> "The woman's relationship to the man is still seen as
> one which may be called "subordination — within —
> equality" ". (Whatever that means)

and

> "Human kind has a common task and dignity within
> creation but the ultimate authority in their partnership
> is vested in the man" (p.7).

Thus, the priesthood requiring qualities of altruism and leadership must by definition be exercised by male persons. Though persons who use this argument are often at pains to say that there is no correlation between the male being the source and him being superior, or more important, this is in fact the necessary consequence of the argument. To be primary and to be secondary indicates a hierarchy of importance. Things which are secondary are, according to the Oxford Dictionary, "next below, coming in place or time after, depending on or derived from, of less importance or originality than what is primary." They are "of the second or inferior rank or class." Thus, the female is not simply "different" but equal; if the male is primary, she is inferior. The point is crucial and is evaded and denied by the opponents of the ordination of women to the priesthood, only because its consequences are so appalling. For few Christians (**there are a few!**) are prepared to believe that God created human beings in terms of their basic gender division, as wholly unequal. Few Christians are prepared to re-write the Genesis myth so glaringly as to say that it was only man and not woman that was created in the image of God (for God cannot be imaged in what is inherently inferior but only by what is essentially perfect).

Out of this fundamental imbalance between the sexes that is ascribed to God's intention, and therefore supported by the Church, has flowed all the discrimination, oppression, vilification and disgust that has been heaped upon women throughout every generation to the detriment of both women and men **and** for the community that they have failed to create. It is this central, causal concept — that God has created the female as inferior, that has allowed the church to rationalise the secular world's behaviour over the centuries towards half the human race. But more psychologically crucial still is the damaged relationship that is thereby created between the feminine and the masculine — the "halved life" to use the Moltmanns' term (Moltmann-Wendel and Moltmann 1991) which affects both the life of the individual woman or man **and** the life of the relationship between them.

> "An individualistic understanding of human beings and
> a mono-theistic understanding of God arose together. If
> we now recognise that human beings form a unity of
> body, soul and spirit and find their salvation in the
> experience of the totality of life, then the image of God
> on earth cannot just be their souls. In their bodily
> nature, in the community of women and men, they

correspond to God. But which God? Surely the God who is rich in relationships, who unites, who forms community, in short the triune God. This God does not rule by dividing and isolating ('divide and rule'), but is present in the union of what is separated and the healing of what is divided. The powerful male may be an imitation of the Almighty, but only a human community can be the image of the triune God, a community in which people have everything in common, apart from their personal characteristics, and share it. This idea helps me to seek God not only above, in heaven, not only deep within my soul, but above all **among us** in our community." (Jurgen Moltmann p.9)

It is in other words, the necessary inter-dependence of the equal but different female and male, both physically and psychologically that creates wholeness within the psyche and wholeness within the systemic relationships which create community, because this interdependence is predicated upon the very nature of the triune God.

The crude biological argument has persisted, even though accurate knowledge of how life in the womb is begun has long since superseded the belief that the male contains within his organs all the components necessary for the creation of new life. The crude biological argument has persisted even though we have long since understood the act of sexual intercourse as involving the **mutual** giving and receiving between man and woman on all levels — physical, emotional and psychological. It has persisted, even though we know that a woman is as likely to initiate sexual activity within a loving relationship, as a man and even though we know that, in a whole variety of ways, the woman may be more active physically than the male within the sexual act itself. Our greater understanding of the range of patterns in physical love-making has widened our understanding of human sexuality generally and this understanding has grown beyond the crude stereo-typing of activities and functions, to a more sophisticated differentiation, to the concept of androgyny, to a more finely tuned yet more uncertain enquiry into all those human qualities hitherto labelled so definitely as "feminine" or "masculine". Far from viewing the two sexes as being properly distinguishable in terms of their psychological and emotional make-up, current research suggests that the greater the degree of integration between "masculine" and "feminine" attributes in both men and women, the greater is the degree of mental and emotional health and maturity of personality (Bem 1977 and Williams 1979).

Since it is inconceivable that God should have created men and women to do other than strive towards wholeness within themselves and between one another, the crude stereo-typing of male and female roles and functions can not any more, I suggest be made the basis for an argument for the stereo-typed roles of the church's ministers. The argument for an all-male priesthood, derived from sexual stereo-typing is therefore also fallacious, and wholly inimitable to the "abundant life" for God's people that God has in mind for them.

We turn now to the second argument towards the ordination of women. Here, the masculine is seen as normative of humanity against which the feminine is compared and, inevitably found wanting. The feminine cannot therefore, it is argued, be used as representational — either of humanity as a whole, as it reaches towards God nor of God in Christ as he reaches out towards humanity. The feminine cannot act representatively in either direction because it is neither normative nor complete. Some of the arguments put forward for the female's "incompleteness" are particularly fascinating. For example, referring again to the Genesis myth, the woman, being fashioned from and taken out of the man is to be regarded as inherently dependent upon him and only made complete through her union with him. Both within the myth itself and in these arguments derived from it, one cannot but wonder if this is a rather obvious example of defensive reversal, since it is clear that mankind in general along with womankind is born of, fashioned from and taken out of woman — not the other way round. (There is of course no argument to be made, pari passu, for claiming the consequent deficiency of the male!)

But the idea and the reality is a fearful one — to be born of woman. And all of us, men and woman alike, may take a lifetime to come to terms with this extraordinary fact of our beginning — the fact that we come out of the body of another. Equally powerful and mysterious is the creative, birth giving act itself, denied to men, which makes women potently creative and therefore to be envied for what a man can never do. It is unsurprising that such potency and such creativity may need to be denied and denigrated in order to make it more manageable.

The only surprise is perhaps that even today, with our more sophisticated psychological knowledge, such blatant oppression and discrimination can be perpetrated against such large numbers of people with so little awareness of its psychological roots.

Some of the arguments that **do** make use of psychological insights reach bizarre conclusions as they seek to establish the inappropriateness of a woman acting representatively as a priest. For example, Russell and Dewey (1978) assert:—

> It is fact, not fantasy, that whereas encounter with a male priest activates in the psychic hinterland of the worshipper, images of great antiquity and power... in the case of the woman priest the images so activated belong to the mother — archetype; and it is now widely

accepted that this image is inimitable to spiritual growth and freedom in those exposed to it. This is so whether the image be of a **positive** type (the consoling, nourishing and protective mother) or **negative** (the devouring or destructive mother). The first enfolds the "child" in a seductive embrace; the second annihilates him as a separate, responsible being. He is either lulled or quelled. That is why a "child" (of whatever age), if he is to grow up, needs a father to lead him away from the blandishments of the "best", as from the tyranny of the "worst", of mothers. (pp 92-3).

Russell and Dewey continue:

"The impact of father-figures belongs, overwhelmingly, not to our infancy but to our childhood, when speech makes possible both verbal communication and rational thought. They speak the Word with authority and (in the normal, creative tensions between the generations) evoke opposition and so the discovery by the child of his own identity. Mother-figures reign in the pre-verbal layers of personality laid down in infancy, where their domination, if it persists, hinders the crucial **psychic** birth, without which one who has not been "re-born" must remain, in some respects infantile.

They conclude:

"At that level (archetypal) a good mother, like a bad mother, must in the end be "bad" for her child, in a fashion not true of even the bad father" (p 94).

It is hard to know where to begin with such a dualistic, unintegrated and disabling analysis. Given that neither Freud nor Jung fully explored the richness of female sexuality and female psychology neither were in fact as dismissive or as bigoted as they have sometimes been made out to be. Moreover, analysts from all schools have, over the years, provided us with a much more rounded and developed understanding of the equally complex and important processes that belong to the feminine psyche. (Feminist analysts such as Chodorow (1978) and Miller (1976) have particularly helped our thinking forward in relation to female psychological development and therefore of the meaning of the feminine). Certainly the biased comments of Russell and Dewey's extrapolation of Jungian thought leaves much more to be said. Rather than the comparative either/or approach which they adopt in comparing the part played by male and female archetypes and of male and female reality figures, we need to acknowledge the necessary and on-going interdependence of each upon the other. Fathers should not be absent in infancy nor children out-grow the influence of mother in later childhood. Each parent supports the child's need of that which the other can offer. Each supports the child's progressively more complex integration of the archetypal formation in his/her unconscious world. The on-going relationship of the parents provide the child with opportunities for a continued oscillation between dependence and autonomy, an oscillation which will continue to be a necessary and healthy part of her/his adult life. And where, as in perhaps 20% of all children's experience in Britain to date there is no second parent for the child, these processes can and must be worked through with other substitute male and female figures.

Part of the difficulties that are displayed with the kind of approach adopted by Russell and Dewey stem from a simplistic equation of regression, dependence and homoeostasis with dysfunction and pathology. But we now understand that such an equation is wholly erroneous. Freud used the term regression in several different ways, only some of which would be regarded as being pathological. Post Freudians and ego psychologists view regression as a necessary process within the operations of the ego. Kris (1952) developed this view-point in an important paper and described a number of ways in which regression in the service of more healthy ego functioning could be better understood. Humour, laughter and play are obvious examples. More importantly we are now much more easily able to understand the healthy necessity of regressing to a dependent position at regular intervals throughout adult life, sometimes for quite prolonged periods. We need to exhibit dependency if we are to be able to seek or receive help in times of stress or crisis and one of the pathological attributes of many professional helpers including the mainly male body of clergy, is that they are so habituated to their role of help-giver that they experience enormous difficulty in becoming a help-seeker. The help seeking activity is in fact often experienced as a greater stressor than the stressful events that prompted it in the first place. Members of the caring professions generally experience particular difficulties in becoming dependent and there is a great deal of truth in old wisdoms such as ''doctors make bad patients''; ''teachers cannot be taught''.

For clergy, the psychological problem of role-strain, which is one way of describing these experiences, is further compounded by a sense that God is the only proper Person on whom to be dependent. Thus, to become dependent upon another person induces guilt as well as shame.

The capacity for mature dependency is essential to the psychological well being of both men and women. Thus, the equation of dependency with inferiority and deficiency is, wholly out of sympathy with our understanding of the nature of adult dependency. The argument however is a crucial one, not only for the eligibility of women to be priests, but on the way the priesthood might be transformed into something more life giving and healthy if women were to be admitted. I would suggest that if women are in general more gifted in the art of mature dependency, then they have a gift of great price to offer to the priesthood. Priests who are more able to model vulnerability, dependency and trust would do great pastoral service to others as well as much for the emotional well being of themselves and their families.

The second set of arguments has also to be understood in terms of what has existed until the last few decades as an unquestioned set of assumptions regarding normative values. These normative values are those of the prevailing dominant culture and are therefore automatically describable in terms of 'masculine' attributes. Since 'masculinity' is dominant, dominant values are 'masculine'. 'Femininity' and the values that are believed to be 'feminine' are measured against these values and found wanting. But as Capra (1982) and others have pointed out, this dominant, thrusting, growth oriented, mechanistic and technological dominant culture is the culture that has produced in this century the holocaust and Hiroshima and high-tech values of every kind. Growth and progress of a continuous kind and at an ever increasing speed, reached perhaps its zenith in our society during the Thatcherite years of the 80's. But, in sharp contrast, we have also seen the different development of what Capra has called the rising culture, focussing interest and concern on quite different values. Ecology and inter-dependence, cooperation and mutuality, intuitiveness and feeling.

In the face of the intractable problems faced by our competitive, militarised, technological, growth oriented society, 'feminine' values are seen by many not merely to be equal but prominent in importance as we approach the end of the 20th century. And as Carr (1991) points out, the feminine is recognised as one of the few coherent, orienting principals of all those groups that go to make up the "New Age". The feminine, far from being inferior, is the essential mode through which humanity and creation can be saved from the "runaway" consequences of masculine values. A female priesthood is wholly syntonic with our current cultural and spiritual needs. It is within this cultural context that both the argument about leadership **and** about representation must be conducted.

But before we arrive at this point, we have to face a transitional difficulty. Generations of secular and spiritual oppression and suppression of the female and the feminine requires urgent re-balancing. Such re-balancing appears to require a counter-balancing superiority of the feminine over the masculine. Few feminists (although some do!) conceive of the ultimate control of the masculine by the feminine as the goal of the struggle and few Christians who support the ordination of women to the priesthood, envisage the replacement of men's control of the Church's structures by women. But the extent to which women have been excluded and marginalised in society and in the Church over the years is the extent to which the transitional period of re-balancing this imbalance will be experienced as shocking and highly disturbing for both women and men alike. Transitional experiences are times of crisis. They are times of rapid, chaotic disequilibrium and are inherently disturbing and shocking but they are also time limited and they require tools and provide experiences that are different from the "plateau" times that occur in between. The plateau that we can expect after the period of transitional crisis will always be different from the plateau that has existed before. In other words, there can be no going back, because the events of the crisis itself will be determinative of change and new experience and this will be incorporated into on going life during the next plateau. The plateau is different from the crisis and it is never easy to predict how those involved most painfully in a psychological and systemic crisis will experience the plateau period which will immediately follow. We can only predict with any certainty that there will have been some movement foward, some movement backward and a new equilibrium discovered which incorporates some of the new and retrieves some of the old.

The Church of England is poised painfully in the midst of the crisis of change. We wait and we prepare for the vote of General Synod. We both participate in and observe the Church as she moved towards the close of 1992 and the next moment of decision. The decision to ordain women as priests is crucially relevant to all the major human concerns that confront us as we approach the year 2000 because it symbolises all the rest. If we can grasp this new moment of opportunity and open the way for our priesthood to become fully human in its male and female members, we will also open the way towards a fuller integration of the crucial partnership between women and men, a re-balancing of which, can alone in human terms, save our planet and its creatures from ultimate disaster and death. For "now, if ever, is the moment for us to redeem the relationship between men and women, to see it as the holiest thing we have, our best possession, a window on eternity, a taste of ecstasy, the inspiration, the splendour, the statement, the root of our humanity." (Furlong 1991, p 154).

Bibliography

Bem, S.L. (1977) "On the utility of alternative procedures for assessing psychological androgyny" (Journal of Consulting and Clinical Psychology, pp 196 -· 205)

Capra, C. (1982) "The Turning Point" (Wildwood Press, London)

Carr, W. (1991) "Manifold Wisdom-Christians in the New Age" (S.P.C.K., London)

Chodorow, N. (1978) The Reproduction of Mothering" (University of California Press, California)

Furlong, M. (1991) "A Dangerous Delight" (S.P.C.K., London)

House of Bishops (1991) "Issues in Human Sexuality" (Church House Press, London)

Kelly, G. (1955) "The Psychology of Personal Constructs" (W.W. Norton, New York)

Kris, E. (1952) "Psychoanalytic Explorations in Art" (International Universities Press, New York)

Miller J.B. (1976) "Toward a New Psychology of Women" (Harmondsworth, Penguin)

Moltmann-Wendel, E and Moltmann, J. (1991) "God-His and Hers" (S.C.M. Press, London)

Russell, G. and Dewey, M. (1978) "Psychological Aspects" (in "Man, Woman and Priesthood" edited by Peter Moore, S.P.C.K., London)

Williams, J.A. (1979) "Psychological Androgyny and mental Health" (in O. Hartnett, G. Boden and M. Fuller, eds., "Women: Sex-Role Stereotyping", Tavistock, London)